Beneath the Cashew Tree

by
Lindaura DaSilva

World rights reserved. This book or any portion thereof may not be copied or reproduced in any form or manner whatever, except as provided by law, without the written permission of the publisher, except by a reviewer who may quote brief passages in a review.

The author assumes full responsibility for the accuracy of all facts and quotations as cited in this book. The opinions expressed in this book are the author's personal views and interpretations, and do not necessarily reflect those of the publisher.

This book is provided with the understanding that the publisher is not engaged in giving spiritual, legal, medical, or other professional advice. If authoritative advice is needed, the reader should seek the counsel of a competent professional.

Copyright © 2014 TEACH Services, Inc.
ISBN-13: 978-1-4796-0260-5 (Paperback)
ISBN-13: 978-1-4796-0261-2 (ePub)
ISBN-13: 978-1-4796-0262-9 (Mobi)
Library of Congress Control Number: 2013954061

Published by

TEACH Services, Inc.
P U B L I S H I N G
www.TEACHServices.com • (800) 367-1844

Acknowledgments

I dedicate this book in loving memory to my parents,
Justiniano and Leonidia, for their outstanding love and care.

I also want to thank my brothers and sisters
and Mark and Phyllis Giambrone for their
words of encouragement as I wrote this book.

Finally, a special thanks to my coworkers
at the Texas Department of Transportation.

Chapter 1

The dust from the gravel road swirled around Lily's car, covering the vehicle in a slight haze. She could hardly believe she was back in Brazil and driving through the familiar valley toward her childhood home. Although it had been more than fifteen years since she had lived there, she knew the area like the back of her hand. This was her farm!

Her eyes darted here and there as she took in the scenery. At the top of the prairie was the house where Lily and her siblings—four sisters and two brothers—had been born. The seven of them had had so much fun growing up together. Lily parked the car underneath the weeping willow tree that she loved to sit under as a child and got out. She moved toward the old wooden gate that was half open, and for a moment she paused and looked to the empty dry meadow. There wasn't much grass, and there weren't any forget-me-not flowers or birds or butterflies in the meadow as she was accustomed to seeing. But then again, there weren't any cattle grazing in the meadow as she remembered.

Although that was different, the same brilliantly blue sky, free of any clouds, was above her, and an aromatic breeze invaded the valley, causing her thoughts to once again return to her childhood, to her peaceful, quiet, happy, and enchanted life on the farm. While resting by the gate, she allowed her mind to wander and fill with cherished memories from the past ….

Mr. Justo walked down the hill with a group of young workers, instructing them on how to use the pruning hook and others tools for the harvest that would start in a few days.

"This will be a good harvest of cacao. I may need to hire more workers and buy a few more good mules for transporting the cocoa beans."

Lily's father was a kind, polite, and friendly man who loved and cared for his farm, which he had received as an inheritance from his parents when he was only eighteen years of age. The farm was his world and his only means of providing for his family.

Mr. Justo was a quiet man of few words who was loved and respected by all the people in the region. He always wore a tailored black, gray, or dark blue suit and a stylish hat. Even when riding on his mule to oversee the work of the farm, he wore his suit or a long-sleeved white shirt.

Cacao was the main source of Mr. Justo's income, as it was for a large population of Brazilians. He expected this harvest to be bountiful! And with the higher price of cacao beans at the world market, Mr. Justo and his employees would surely benefit from a plentiful harvest. Mr. Justo didn't have the largest farm in the area, but the soil was fertile, and in addition to the cacao crop, the farm grew a variety of fruits and vegetables. Mr. Justo was excited about the prospects of a prosperous year, because he had dreams for his children that he wanted to accomplish.

Mr. Justo had stopped to look at something while the worked continued walking. But the group stopped when they spotted an old ragged man approached them.

"I need to speak to the owner of the farm," begged the aged man to the group of workers.

"You, old man! Who do you think you are looking for work here at this farm?" one man said.

"The boss is coming," said another worker, shutting up the loudmouth of the group.

It was not difficult for the elderly man to identify the owner of the farm.

"Good afternoon, sir, I came from far away and have sought work throughout the region, but every farmer says they no longer need any more workers, or there are no job openings. I know I am an old man, but do you have a job for me? Please, boss! I have lots of energy, and I am in desperate need of a job."

Mr. Justo patiently listened to the man present his case. "Yes, I do have work for you to do. Please make yourself comfortable while I go get some extra tools. Also, if you are hungry, my wife can give you something to eat."

"Thank you very much, sir. You have a good heart. I have heard about your kindness from others in the area. May the Lord bless you and your family. Thank you, thank you, thanks you!" The old man repeated his message of gratitude the best way he could.

For the rest of the afternoon, others workers straggled onto the property and asked to speak with Mr. Justo. He took the time to talk with each of them before giving them a set of tools, instructions, and some groceries. The workers came from all different places. Many of them had walked a great distance in search of work, carrying only a worn-out burlap bag with very few belongings inside. There were those who were accompanied by many children, and a young pregnant woman showed up with her husband. The last two employees hired were a man and his wife, who happened to be a midwife, which came in handy, for she went to work that very night helping to deliver the young pregnant woman's baby!

The workers were hired, and the harvesting would soon begin.

Chapter 2

A few days had passed, maybe a week, and everything was ready and organized for the cacao harvest. With all of the new field hands at the farm, a teacher from the capital city had been hired to teach at the farm school and keep the children occupied as the men worked.

The men looked forward to the harvest for the money it would bring in. On the other hand, the children looked forward to the harvest because of the excitement of the special celebrations that accompanied the harvest. There were special school essays to write and folklore to be shared and school parties.

It was the first day of the harvest. Lily and her siblings sat around the table waiting for breakfast Felipe said, "Mother, I want to see the men harvest the cacao."

Nydia moved toward the table with plates of couscous, cheese, chocolate, and a jug of milk. She set the food down on the large wooden table before addressing her son's request.

"No one is allowed inside the outback of cacao during this period of the harvest unless you are going to work," she said.

"I'd like to work and earn a salary, but father only gives me clothes, shoes, and—"

"And food," Mother quickly pointed out to Tony, her oldest son. "On second thought, Tony, you will help your father tomorrow after school, but no one else has my permission to enter the outback of cacao."

"Why, Mother?" Lily asked

"Because you children hinder the progress of the workers by distracting the men from their job. Also, if one of you gets lost among the cacao trees, all work would have to stop to search for you, which was disappoint and disgrace your father. Now, please, eat your breakfast."

Lily remained quiet, letting her mind wander and imagining what the harvest must be like in the outback, which was thick with cacao trees. *If only I could have a quick peek*, she thought.

"And you, baby, what are you thinking?" Mother whispered to Lily, who was staring off into space.

"Oh, nothing," Lily responded, not wanting to share her desires with her mother right then.

"Eat your couscous, my dear," Mother said, letting the matter drop as to the subject of Lily's obvious daydreaming episode.

Lily was the youngest of the family and was spoiled rotten. She had difficulties speaking, so Mother devoted a lot of attention to her care and education at home. Mother would spend hours helping Lily talk, initiating conversations with her, telling her stories, and teaching her songs and poems.

As Lily ate her food, she looked out the window and watched the workers pass by the front porch as they headed out to the outback. Her father treated his workers well. As a special welcome to everyone on the first day of the harvest, they all received breakfast and lunch, which included cooked yucca and pieces of fried dried beef.

Lily slipped off her chair at the table and moved toward the front porch. Once outside in the fresh air, she eagerly watched the procession of workers headed for the outback. The farm was quite large, with several cacao outbacks, each having a different name. She intently tried to pay attention to which direction they were headed in hopes of following the same trail if the opportunity arose to sneak away and survey the harvest herself.

Losing sight of the men from her vantage point on the porch, Lily descended the steps and began following them at a distance down one of the trails. However, she did not get far when a neighbor from the valley who was looking for Mr. Justo called out to Lily for assistance. As she turned to see who was speaking to her, she lost sight of the workers and the direction they were headed.

Lily went in search of her father. Upon finding him, she said, "Father, one of our neighbors is here, and he wants to speak to you."

Once Mr. Justo and Lily were within earshot of the neighbor, the man began speaking. "Good morning, Mr. Justo. I'm sorry for bothering you so early in the morning, but my donkey is sick, and I do not know what to do. It is a young animal, and I don't want to lose him. Do you have any medicine that might help him?"

"Don't apologize. We are neighbors, and we are here to help each other. I just bought some medicine from the veterinary for some of my farm animals. Maybe that will help your donkey feel better. It is certainly worth a try. Let me go get the medicine, and I will come with you to look at your donkey."

"Father, may I go with you?" Lily begged, a sparkle in her eyes. All thoughts of the harvest were gone as her mind began thinking of this new adventure with her father. "Please, father, please. I want to go see the donkey."

Mr. Justo could not resist her appeals and, since it would help his wife with their youngest child, he said yes.

Lily was an active and curious child who was always ready for an activity or outing. She had an enormous amount of energy, and she loved to explore her surroundings at Good Vision Farm. The new teacher at the school was not accepting students in pre-K, so Lily was left home while her siblings went to school on the other side of the valley across the river.

Mr. Justo returned to the house to tell his wife that he was taking Lily with him to a neighbor's house to help him with his donkey. He then disappeared in search of the medicine. Lily ran around the yard as she waited for her father to get back. She was eager to go see the donkey. She jumped up and down and clapped her hands when she saw Father come walking toward them with the bottle of medicine in his hand.

Lily knew the way to her neighbor's house, so she ran ahead of the two men. She practically flew down the hill. She loved the feel of the wind rushing through her hair. Father and the neighbor walked behind her, their long legs making up the distance in no time compared to her little legs, even though she was running.

As the men got closer, she heard the neighbor say, "Do you see that weeping willow tree over there? That is where my donkey is lying."

Lily squinted in the bright sun, trying to see the donkey, but the tall grass made it hard to see. So she ran a little faster, trying to get to the animal before the men did.

"Lily, wait up please," her father called as they grew closer to the weeping willow tree. Lily obeyed and waited for her father. When he caught up to her, he reached down and took her hand, and they walked the rest of the way together.

The poor donkey looked very ill. Mr. Justo knelt down beside the animal and stroked its head. Although he was not a trained veterinarian, his years of experience as a farmer had taught him what he needed to know about the care of animals. He examined the animal very carefully before sharing his thoughts with his neighbor.

"Friend, your animal is malnourished, and it appears that it has eaten something that has given it stomach cramps, as its abdomen is very tight. But don't worry, the medicine I brought with me should help, and your animal should be well in no time."

"It is too bad that this happened today, Mr. Justo. You see, I was on my way to the fairground this morning with the intention of selling my donkey when it wouldn't budge and lay down on the ground. Since I was not too far from your farmhouse, I came to see if you could help. I appreciate your help, but I don't think I can sell my donkey today in this condition, unless of course, you would like to purchase it, sir? I would sell it to you really cheap since you helped to save its life."

"But I have no need of a donkey. What I am currently looking for is a good team of mules."

"Please, sir. This donkey is a good worker and has the 'patience of Job.' It will make a good companion."

At this point, the two men smiled. All donkeys have the "patience of Job." Lily didn't understand the joke. Instead, she piped up and said, "'Patience of Job.' Yes, Job is his name. But because he is still young, I will call him Joey."

Lily knelt down beside "Joey" and began stroking the donkey's head. With the extra attention and the medicine flowing through his system, Joey began to stir and after a little while he stood up, much to Lily's delight. She cheered for Joey and exclaimed that his speedy recovery was a miracle!

Mr. Justo watched Lily hug Joey's neck and talk to him like he was an old friend. The joy that the donkey was clearly bringing to his youngest child was excuse enough to buy the animal.

"OK, neighbor. I guess I will buy the donkey, since he and Lily seem to have bonded."

At this announcement, Lily jumped up and down and clapped her hands, excitedly telling Joey, "You are coming home with me. We are going to be best friends!"

Mr. Justo and the neighbor agreed upon a price before parting. On the way back home, Lily led Joey by a halter rope while her father walked beside them. As they walked, Lily asked question after question about donkeys and how to care for them. Father patiently told her everything he knew about donkeys. He told her when to feed Joey and what kind of foods to give him. He also told her what he knew about the habit and various breeds of donkeys. Mixed in with the educational tidbits, he shared funny stories and experiences he had had with donkeys.

"Some people think that donkeys are stubborn," Father said, "but they are smart animals and can be quite affectionate toward their owners."

As he finished speaking, Joey let out a loud cry. *Hee-haw!*

"Does Joey know what we are saying?" Lily asked.

"Maybe Joey was just affirming that you have won his friendship and trust," Father joked.

You two laughed at the thought that Joey could really understand what they were saying, and the three continued to trudge up the hill toward their home.

When they arrived in the front yard and Lily caught sight of her mother, she called out, "Look, Mother! Father bought me a present! His name is Joey. He was sick, but he is much better now. I will let him rest under the mango tree until the kids get home from school."

"Very well, Lily. I was just commented in the kitchen how I need more help to get the pure water from the waterfall up to the house, and now help has arrived in the form of a donkey! Remember that you must share your donkey with your brothers and sisters like Marie does with her cow, Bananinha. The cow belongs to all, so will Joey."

Lily could hardly wait for her brothers and sisters to return from school. To pass the time, she played outside near the mango tree so that she could be near Joey. She talked to him, petted him, and brought him big clumps of grass for him to munch on. Finally, after what seemed like forever, it was almost time for school to be out. Lily asked Mother for permission to go meet the kids, and once granted, she took off down the hill toward the school. Lily was huffing and puffing by the time she reached the school. She leaned up against the building to catch her breath. She had just enough time to rest when the school bell rang, and her siblings, along with the other kids from school, came flooding out the door.

"What are you doing here, Lily?" Felipe asked.

"There is a surprise at home," Lily exclaimed. "It is a big surprise. I can't wait for you to see it."

Lily grinned from ear to ear, and her excitement was contagious. Soon all of the children were jumping up and down and asking question after question, trying to get Lily to tell them what the surprise was.

"You will have to wait and see for yourselves," she informed them.

With that, all of the children took off running for the farm. Lily did her best to catch up with them, but the older kids were much faster. But since the kids didn't know what the surprise was or where it was hidden, everyone slowed down and waited for Lily at the top of the hill.

Once Lily reached the group, she joyfully led them to where Joey was still resting under the mango tree. "Here is my present! His name is Joey."

"A donkey!?!" the kids shrieked with laughter. "This is your big surprise?"

"It would be a better surprise if it was a cow like mine," said Marie.

"Or a pony or horse," said Pitanga, the granddaughter of Karuru the Indian.

"What is wrong with Joey?" Lily asked in a defensive tone of voice.

"Donkeys are stupid, stubborn, silly, and slow," one of the kids said.

"That is not true," Lily shot back. "I will provide to you that Joey is smart. Then you will apologize to me and Joey. My father said that donkeys are not stubborn; they are just cautious."

The kids continued to laugh.

Lily had been so excited, but now her feelings were hurt. The kids wouldn't stop laughing or teasing her about Joey.

Mother had heard the whole conversation and stepped in to defend her young daughter. "Children, donkeys really are smart animals. They are also loyal companions, reliable workers, and are friendly creatures. And think about this. In history famous kings and generals rode upon donkeys. Jesus rode into the city of Jerusalem on a donkey, and a crowd of people with palm branches in their hands shouted 'Hosanna to the son of David. Hosanna!'"

The children quieted down and some of them looked at their feet as they listened to her talk about the many good qualities that donkeys possess. After she was done speaking, she invited the children onto the porch for a snack.

Lily loved her mother and was so glad that she told the other children all of the good qualities of donkeys just as Father had shared with her. Her bubble had been momentarily popped, but it soon filled again with happy thoughts of the adventures that she was sure to have with her new friend Joey.

Chapter 3

Lily loved mornings on the farm. She always woke up early. In fact, her mother used to say that she got up with Zeze the rooster.

As soon as Lily's eyes popped open, she would hop out of bed, quickly dress herself and brush her teeth, and then run out the door into the front yard and begin throwing corn and bran to the chickens and chicks. After that she would run down the hill to the corral, climb the fence, and watch the cows being milked. The milk was poured into large aluminum containers and brought to the kitchen to be processed and distributed. After the milking was done, Lily would run uphill toward the house, racing against the clock, for she wanted to be back when her father blew the whelk shell at seven o'clock, announcing that it was time for all of the workers to head to the fields. The whelk shell was yellowish in color and emitted a loud, prolonged sound that could be heard for miles when her father blew on it.

Mr. Justo blew the shell twice a day, announcing the beginning and end of the workday. One day when Mr. Justo had blown the shell, he noticed that Lily and her sisters were staring at him with a certain curiosity. He realized that he had never explained where the sound came from, so he called the children closer, showed them how to blow and where the sound came from, and told them the importance of that simple whelk shell as a form of communication.

"Not only is the shell blown to announce the beginning and end of work, but we also blow the shell to signal the start of many special events such as church worship, weddings, and emergencies," Father told his little audience. "This shell was brought up from the bottom of the sea, and it is the perfect shape to make a wonderful horn."

The children continued to stare at him and the shell. "Now, why are you all still looking at me with big eyes? It wouldn't be because you want to blow the shell, would it?"

Lily and her siblings vigorously nodded their heads up and down.

"Very well, very well," Father said. "I will teach you how to blow the shell on the weekend, but please do not try to blow it without my permission."

The children were tempted to blow the shell when they saw it in the house, but they knew better than to disobey their father. An act of disobedience would not be tolerated in the family. Although Mother was devoted to her children and their well being, even getting up at midnight to light a fire to make some tea or warm milk for a sick child, she would not stand for her children disrespecting the word of their parents.

The cacao harvest was in full swing, but Lily had forgotten about the excitement of the harvest and her desire to explore the outback since she had Joey to play with. She spent all of her spare time with the donkey. One day as she was trying to teach Joey a new trick, Manolo passed by her guiding a few mules loaded down with the white seeds of the cacao, which would be dried in the wooden greenhouse. The oven-setter was responsible for the drying process. On the first floor of the building were two clay ovens, and on the second floor the seeds would be spread out on the wooden floor. The oven-setter had to keep the temperature of the wood fire just right to dry the cacao beans before they could be sold.

"Oh no, Manolo. I completely forgot about the harvest! Has it already come to an end?" Lily asked.

"No, Lily," Manolo responded with a chuckle. "We still have a long way to go before the harvest is done. Today we are at the cascade outback."

Her curiosity was once again piqued, and her mind began racing as she thought of a way to sneak to the outback and view the workers harvesting the cacao. Now was not the time because her sisters would be returning from school at any moment, which meant that there were more people keeping an eye out for her. She determined that she would look at the situation tomorrow morning.

The next morning after her siblings headed off to school, Lily began planning her adventure to the outback. As she sat thinking about her next move, she saw a young man leading Joey down the path toward the waterfall with wooden buckets to fetch water for the workers. Lily knew the waterfall was in the middle of the forest. In a split second, she decided that this was her chance. Lily ran to catch up to the young man while keeping enough distance between them so that he would not see her and send her back home.

Lily followed behind Joey as they went downhill from the house and then turned on a narrow path between the trees. As they entered the forest, it was as if a curtain was opened before her eyes. *This is beautiful,* she thought.

The accumulation of leaves that had fallen from the cacao trees over the years formed a fluffy carpet with several layers of red, pink, yellow, and brown leaves covering the trail. The cacao's outback was dense and dark. The large trees of the outback stretched toward the sky, shading and protecting the cacao trees and creating a sense of mystery in the darkened forest. Lily's eyes grew wider as she gazed at the beautiful cacao trees were their yellow, green, and red fruit and the buds that were still popping out on the trunk and branches.

The sun shone between the leaves of the trees in patches, making the dewdrops on the bananas tree leaves sparkle and shimmer. Lily almost blurted out, "Look at that!" when she saw a large spider web that was about two yards in diameters, but she knew she had to keep quiet if she wanted to go deeper into the outback.

This is wonderful! she thought.

A little further into the woods, a cicada practiced its recital, followed by a cricket, and then a frog and a variety of birds. The finishing touch to the symphony of nature was the rushing sound of the waterfall. Lily had never seen or heard anything so beautiful than the symphony of nature that was surrounding her. Its purity, simplicity, and originality were spectacular. The plants, flowers and little forest creatures and insects all seemed to be participating in the joy of the moment. Lost in her thoughts as her eyes took in all the sights and her ears absorbed all of the sounds, she didn't realize that she had stopped walking. After several minutes, Lily looked up and realized that she was alone in the woods. Joey and the young man were nowhere in sight.

Lily walked a bit further down the trail before realizing that the sun was climbing in the sky and she better head back home. Time had passed too quickly. As Lily paused in the trail, she heard the *swoosh* and the *thwack* of the workers long, sharp pruning hooks. She turned to look in all directions, and it was then that she noticed an opening in the trees and a group of workers cutting the stems of the fruit as it hung from the cacao tree. She crept forward and peeking through the leaves. Some workers were cutting the fruit off the tree while others collected the fruit and placed them in heaping piles. Still other workers cut the fruit open and placed the seeds on beds of banana leaves to drain the excess juice.

I accomplished my mission, Lily thought. *I safely made it to the outback to see the harvest, but now I must return home.* Since she had not deviated off the main trail, she was sure that she could make it home without any problems. Lily turned around and began heading back in the direction that she had come in. When she was more than halfway home, Lily heard a strange noise in the forest. It sounded as if someone was moving slowly so as not to make a sound stepping on the dried leaves. Lily stopped, and the sound stopped. Lily moved, and the sound resumed. She shuddered with fright and took off running as fast as her legs would carry her.

She ran with all her might until she burst out of the forest into the blazing sunlight. But she didn't stop there. She continued to run until she was underneath the safety of the cashew tree. Lily loved sitting under the cashew tree. It was a safe haven to her and a good place to go think and play. Beneath its broad branches and green leaves, she finally stopped to catch her breath.

Her breathing had just returned to normal when Mother emerged from around the house.

"Lily, where have you been? It isn't funny to hide from your mother! I have been looking for you all morning! Now come indoors!"

Mother was so upset that she didn't wait for Lily to answer her question about Lily's whereabouts. Instead, she took the girl instead and assigned her chores to do to keep her busy and told her that she couldn't go outside for the rest of the day because she had scared her mother so badly. However, Mother never questioned Lily further.

Chapter 4

Lily didn't tell her mother about the strange noise she heard on the trail because she knew if she did she would be disciplined for disobeying. Lily followed Mother inside and saw that she had been working on a patchwork quilt.

"Come help me pick some prints for the quilt from the material your grandmother sent us," Mother said, pointing to the various fabric stacked in a bundle.

Lily and Mother worked for a time in silence before Lily asked, "Mother, is it true that Monster Caipora is real?"

"Where did you hear that name?" Mother asked in surprise.

"Pitanga, the granddaughter of Indio Karuru, told me the story."

"I do not want to hear you repeat that name ever again. That story is purely superstitious and deals with the Indians' pagan gods."

"What is a pagan, Mother?" Lily asked.

"A pagan is a person who does not believe in the God of heaven. Pagans base their faith on magical arts, and they worship several gods and goddess rather than the one true God."

"How many gods and goddesses do they believe in?" Lily asked.

"I don't know; maybe hundreds. Pagans often worship aspects of nature. For example, many people worship Mother Earth. They believe that this planet is the creator and sustainer of life. The elements of the earth—air, fire, and water—have special significance to pagans. Furthermore, pagans are often involved in witchcraft."

"Witchcraft is really bad, isn't it, Mother?" Lily asked, her eyes wide with fear.

"Yes, it is."

"Where do pagans live, Mother?"

"Pagans are everywhere. They form small and large groups. They practice witchcraft in secret places and in public. Some of their practices include worshiping idols, participating in human sacrifice, and talking to the spirit world. Pagans have been deceived by Satan and are enemies of Jesus Christ. They have fallen into the same trap that Eve fell into in the Garden of Eden. We must stay close to God and follow His commands so that we don't get tricked into believing the lies of the devil," Mother said.

Mother paused in her speech and looked directly into Lily's eyes. "You need to understand, Lily. This is so important. We believe in God, Creator of the heavens and the earth. We are His children, made in His own image. Do you believe that?"

"Yes, Mother. You know I believe that God created all the beautiful things I see. Since I was a baby, you've taught me that that is what the Bible says."

Lily took a breath and then, with a puzzled look on her face, asked a question. "Mother, do you have a Bible?"

"No, I do not have a Bible."

"How do you believe what the Bible says if you don't have a Bible to read?" Before Mother could answer her question, a thought popped into Lily's mind and she said, "When I learn to read, I will find a Bible and read to you."

Once again, before Mother could say something, Lily fired off another question. "Mother, why…"

"You are the most talkative girl I know," Mother said, interrupting Lily's last question. "I hope that you will learn to read really soon."

Since Lily was the youngest and the last child at home, she and Mother had a special bond. In addition to their love for one another, they shared facial resemblance, they liked and sang the same songs, and they both had the same taste in books. They liked stories, books, and magazines. That afternoon, reading the Bible was added to their list of things to do together.

Lily helped Mother around the house and played with her siblings once they got home from school, but she could not forget about the strange sound she had heard among the cacao trees. That night as she lay in bed, Lily could not sleep. The thought of that strange sound kept her awake.

She longed to tell one of her sisters about the adventure in the heart of the plantation and see if they had any idea what the strange noise was, but she wasn't sure if she could trust any of them to keep her secret.

Leah, the eldest sister, was a perfect teenager. She never disobeyed her parents and was a model child. If Lily told her, she figured that sooner or later Leah would spill the beans and tell her parents.

Then there was Marie. She was a good sister and a very nice girl. Lily could count on her for almost everything. However, Marie thought she was Father's favorite child. Lily could not take the risk of telling Marie her secret, for Marie would surely tell Father.

Lily considered her third sister, Meg, for she was rebellious and bold. She often challenged their parents. Lily figured that Meg would be willing to go to the woods and look for clues as to the source of the mysterious sound. However, Lily feared that Meg would then turn on her and share her secret with Mother.

That just left Tina, her fourth sister. She was a secret keeper. Lily knew she would not tell Mother if Lily were to confide in Tina. And she did like scary, mysterious things, because she was always listening to her best friend Pitanga tell her strange tales of ancient folklore.

All of these thoughts tumbled through Lily's mind as she drifted off to sleep.

With each passing week, more and more sacks were stacked at the greenhouse, where they waited for transport to the large export warehouse in the city.

The harvest was going well, and Mr. Justo was very happy. He hoped that he could accomplish his dream of bringing in a large harvest that would supply enough money for his children to go to college when they were ready. The greenhouse was already full, so that was a good sign. With no more room to store the sacks of cacao beans, he decided to take the beans to the exportation warehouse and sell them. It was a lot of work to load up the 200 sacks of cacao beans on a large troop of mules, but everyone was excited to see the first load of beans head to town to be sold. All of their hard work was about to pay off. Once the caravan was all loaded, the grand procession to the market began.

This was the first of many trips to the city, because the harvest continued for more than six months. It was a busy, but exciting, time on the farm. Each person, including the children, had something to do. Lily loved her assigned task. It was her duty to feed the chickens. Of course, she also took time to play with the chicks. As she held the chicks and touched their downy features, Zeze strutted around the yard, jealous of his hens and chicks and the fact that someone was showing them so much attention.

One day as Lily and Zeze were running around in the front yard, an intruder prowled nearby. A fox hid in the bushes and waited for the right moment to attack the chickens, where were hatching their eggs in the coop.

Lily was happily skipping around the yard chasing Zeze when the rooster started crowing and making a distinctive series of clucks to attract the attention of Lily and the hens. The commotion caused Lily to turn around and look in all directions. At this point, the chickens clucked in panic and flapped their wings in defense as they spied a huge red fox creeping toward them with his sharp teeth gleaming in the sunlight.

There was no time to lose. Lily had to act fast. She looked around for something she could use to scare away the fox. It was then that she saw the feeding dish containing some grains of corn. She ran toward it, picked it up, aimed at her target, and threw it in the face of the fox. The dish hit its intended target on the head and the corn scattered all around. The fox bolted away into the bushes, disappearing as quickly as it had appeared.

"Go away and look for other food, smelled old fox!" Lily yelled after the retreating animal.

Zeze pranced around the yard with his wings spread wide. It was as if he were saying thank you to Lily for saving his hens and chicks. Instead of chasing Lily away, he now came close and let Lily caress his head and neck. From that day on Lily and Zeze were good friends.

Lily was thankful for the love and care of her parents and the friendship of her siblings, but she was also grateful for the companionship of the animals on the farm that she played with every day and that kept her company while everyone was busy going to school or working. Life was good on the farm with her family and animal friends.

Chapter 5

Lily had forgotten about the strange noise until one day when she was picking wild flowers near the edge of the woods. She stopped in her tracks and listened. *It has to be the fox*, she thought.

Instead of being scared, a determination to scare the fox away and protect the animals on the farm came over Lily, and she looked around for a big stick. She planned to hit the fox so hard that he would never come back to the farm. As she was quietly creeping forward, a man in his twenties suddenly emerged from the bushes.

"Urucuia! What are you doing here? You scared me!"

The man stared at Lily, and she realized that he was not Urucuia, the Indian's grandson. He was a complete stranger. Lily tried to scream, but no sound came out of her mouth. She wanted to run away, but her legs would not move. Lily tried to remain calm as the stranger moved closer toward her.

"Do not ask me what I am doing here, little girl! I can be here if I want to because this is my farm!" the stranger said in a loud voice.

"This is not your farm! Our family owns this farm. I am going to tell my father about you," Lily shot back.

The man's face turned red and he grew angry at Lily's defiance. Lily shrank back in fear of what might happen next, but all of a sudden the man was running away down the hill toward the main road. Lily turned to see what had caused the man to flee, and saw Joey running full speed away chasing the mean man off the property.

Life suddenly seemed quite complicated and scary. The initial secret of exploring the woods and hearing the strange sound had turned into a potentially dangerous situation with a stranger roaming the farm. Lily had to find a way to talk to her sisters.

Lily played indoors for the rest of the day, only coming outside later in the afternoon to watch the "cattle parade" as the animals came home for the night. Every evening at the same time, even when the rain fell in torrents and the sun dipped lower in the sky, the cattle made their way home to spend the evening near the house. The cattle would be grazing in the pastures, but at the "correct" time they would walk single file to their nightly gathering place. It happened every day. Lily and her siblings liked watching the "cattle parade" from the second floor windows of the greenhouse.

At supper that evening, Father said he was going to the village in the morning and would not return for a couple of days. He had a wedding to perform and a minor legal hearing to deal with. Mr. Justo was an appointed justice of the peace and the only judge for that region. It was his duty to perform marriages and listen to court proceedings when the need arose. He was an excellent judge, and the people appreciated his honesty and wisdom.

Before leaving for the village the next day, Father ordered his workers to take the remained sacks of cacao beans from the greenhouse and store them beside the pantry in the house for safe keeping. Many of the workers were going to the village for the weekend to enjoy the festivities at the fairground, and Father wanted to make sure the rest of the harvest was safe before taking it to the city to sell. Once the harvest was secure, Father bid his family goodbye and left for the village.

With Father off on his own adventure, Mother decided to make the day extra special for the children. They played hide and seek and tag and planned a talent show, with Mother as the host. It was a quiet late, around ten o'clock, when everyone went to sleep. Lily had fallen asleep in the hammock when Leah took her to bed.

Lily was groggy and half asleep, but she remembered that she had had something very important to tell her sister. Unfortunately, with the excitement of last evening and today, she had completely forgot to share the startling news of the stranger whom she had met near the woods.

"I saw a strange man near our house, Leah! I meant to tell someone last night, but I forgot. He was very mean," Lily whispered.

"There is no strangers are the farm. It was probably Urucuia," her sister said.

"No, Leah! It was not Urucuia. He was a stranger. I know!"

"Be quiet, Lily. Go to sleep!" Leah said as she tucked Lily into bed.

Lily was so tired that she didn't argue with Leah. She simply shut her eyes and fell fast asleep.

As usual, Mother was the last one to go to bed, and in a few minutes she was asleep. However, she wasn't asleep for long when she was awakened by a loud noise near the kitchen door. After having seven children, she was a light sleeper.

Why is someone at the back door? she thought. Then she remembered the sacks of cacao beans in the storage room near the pantry. *Someone is trying to break into our house and steal the beans!* She jumped out of bed, ran to the boys' bedroom, and shook them awake; then she ran to the girls' bedroom and took Lily in her arms. Everyone was scared to death. The girls held back screams as they heard the intruder trying to kick open the back door.

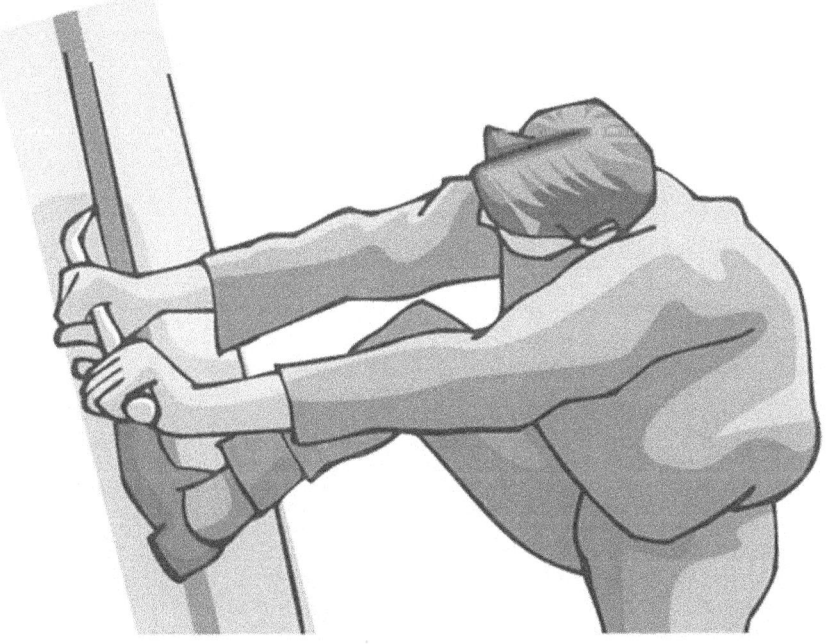

"What are we going to do, Mother?" the girls asked through their tears.

"We have a machete, Mother. Let's hope that the intruder gets inside. Then we can strike him with the machete," Tony said. He was certainly more courageous and brave than any of the others.

As they stood huddled together trying to figure out what to do, Lily wiggled free from her mother's grasp, ran to the living room, grabbed the whelk shell, and blew it for all she was worth. And she kept blowing it until she heard the sound of the workers who were still on the property rushing toward the house. The workers showed up with candles, gas lamps, knives, and machetes in their hands. They knew something serious was going on because the shell was blown at midnight.

As soon as people began running up the hill, the intruder fled the scene. Some of the workers investigated every inch of the yard looking for clues. They could see footprints of a man's shoes and the kitchen door was definitely damaged from the kicking.

It was hard to sleep after such a scary experience, but eventually all of the workers went home and Mother and the children returned to their beds. The question on everyone's mind as they drifted off into a restless sleep was "Who was the intruder?" Was he someone from the village or perhaps even a neighbor? No one knew, but hopefully Father would know what to do when he got home.

Chapter 6

The next morning a messenger was sent to find Mr. Justo and tell him about the intruder. As soon as he performed the wedding ceremony, he came home to the farm. After checking on the well being of his family, he called a meeting with his employees to see if any of them could provide some clues as to who the intruder was.

"Thank you for coming to this very important meeting," Mr. Justo began. "I also want to thank you for the protection and care that you showed my family last night. I praise God that no one was hurt. I wanted to meet together to see if any of you witnessed anything suspicious earlier in the day or yesterday evening that may help us determine who the intruder was."

Marieta, the oven-setter's wife, immediately raised her hand. Once Mr. Justo acknowledged her, she blurted out. "I saw Urucuia around the main house last evening."

"I also saw him last night," Matildes said. "Urucuia was in the front yard, but he may have gone to the back yard later on."

Urucuia was in the crowd, and upon hearing two people testify against him, he shouted, "I am not a thief, neither am I an intruder!"

"If you are not a thief, what did you do last night?"

"I … I'm not a burglar!" Urucuia did not provide concrete evidence as to his whereabouts the previous evening, but it did not appear that he was the burglar with leather shoes.

The meeting began to get out of hand, and everyone's voices rose to a higher level. Lily anxiously looked around, but she knew she needed to speak up, so she approached her father and said, "Father, please don't be angry with me, but I saw a strange man hiding in the bushes around the house the other day."

"And you didn't say anything?" exclaimed her mother.

"Calm down," Father said. "Now tell me, what did this man look like?"

"He was young. He looked scary with a potbelly and a long, thick nose. I also remember that he was wearing leather boots."

After hearing those descriptions of the man, Mr. Justo dismissed the meeting. He already had an idea of who the possible burglar could be. As the employees left, they knew Mr. Justo would take care of the situation. As a judge, he knew how to handle these things.

Father was glad that Lily had told the truth. But he was also a little disappointed, for he hoped that he had taught his children to come to him right away about any problem they were having or anything out of the ordinary that they did not understand. Father loved his children so much, and he wanted to have a relationship with them. He wanted to train, guide, and discipline them in love. It was his desire that they would obey him because of their love for him. By raising his children in this manner, he hoped to impress upon them obedience and love for their heavenly Father as well.

Lily had let him down by disobeying his orders to not go into the outback and then by not telling him about the stranger; however, no matter how many times the children failed, disappointed, or hurt him, he chose to forgive them and shower them with love, for he wanted to model for them the love of God and show them compassion and mercy.

Mother had the same philosophy in raising the children as Father did. She encouraged them, corrected them, and loved them. She taught them right from wrong and instructed them in the ways of God. Although Mother didn't know much about the Bible, she believed in a God in heaven, and she believed in doing good instead of evil.

Both Father and Mother reminded the children that they should always obey their parents. They all could learn a lot from this incident: lessons in obedience, honesty, and trust. Mother and Father also realized that they gave Lily too much freedom for her age, and they needed to keep a closer eye on their youngest child.

After Father was assured the everything was alright, he headed back to the city to hear a case at the courthouse. He promised to return as quickly as possible, and he promised to bring something special for the children upon his return. The children anxiously awaited Father's return, for they knew he would keep his word and bring back a surprise.

When Father did return home from the hearing at the courthouse, he brought many gifts. He brought beautiful colored fabrics for Mother, ribbons and headbands for the girls, cowboy hats for the boys, and a large wrapped box for Lily. Lily opened the box and found coloring books, colored pencils, an ABC book, and other school materials.

Lily squealed in delight at all of the wonderful supplies. "From now on I will be teaching you reading and writing here at home every morning," Father told her.

"Really, Father! Oh, thank you. I love everything," Lily exclaimed.

With the rest of her siblings at school, and her parents busy on the farm, it was clear to Mother and Father that Lily needed more supervision and activities to keep her busy and out of trouble. Hence, their idea of devoting some time each day to her education.

Lily was young and had much to learn about obedience and making wise decisions, but she had loving parents who were committed to training her in the ways of the Lord.

Chapter 7

The purpose of teaching Lily at home was to keep her indoors and to motivate her to learn to read and write and do basic arithmetic. In addition, Lily asked to learn some about science, music, and art. Mother included social behavior as an integral part of her education. Everyone knew that Lily was in preschool, but she thought she was in elementary school. She took school seriously and tried to imitate her sisters by following the schedule of the farm's school.

After Lily was finished with her lessons and schoolwork, she often waited on the front porch for her siblings and the other farm kids to return from school. Some days she would play under the cashew tree as she waited. It was a unique cashew tree that was about twelve yards tall and had branches that grew toward the ground instead of stretching up to the sky. The branches actually touched the ground and poured out roots as if they were another tree. The strong and straight trunk was divided by four principal branches that boasted a large, green canopy. The cashew tree simultaneously produced the three colors of fruit: gray, red, and yellow.

The cashew tree was planted in the middle of the prairie in front of the main house. It was a beautiful tree that served as a perfect play spot for Lily and her siblings and the other children on the farm. They would dream under that tree, climb its branches, and play all sorts of imaginary games. Beneath the cashew tree's canopy, the kids felt protected and secure.

When the kids finally came home from school that day, they excitedly talked about the upcoming school play in which Tony and Marie were the main performers and Leah and Paloma, her best friend, were to dance. Lily looked forward to the play and excitedly chattered about it for days until the event finally took place.

The performance was colorful and funny, and everyone in attendance laughed and clapped for the children. After the play Urucuia approached Paloma and offered her a violet flower wrapped in a love note. Of course, Lily could not let that moment pass without asking what was in the note.

"Paloma, what does the note say?" Lily asked.

"Lily, it is none of your business," Paloma responded.

"I can imagine what it says. You and Urucuia are falling in love! Lovers, lovers," Lily chanted.

Hoping to quiet her, Urucuia tossed a chocolate bonbon into Lily mouth. Of course, as soon as he did so, he regretted it because the candy had been for Paloma,

Urucuia was a very neat young man. His mother was a native Indian woman who was very attractive, and his father was a white European who went back to his country with the intention to return, but never did. Urucuia had the skin color, the eyes, the social culture, and the moral beliefs of his father. He never participated in the Indians rituals or celebrations. He did not like the dances, and he hated the drums that were used in the many rituals. He believed in God, the supreme Creator of the earth and humanity. Urucuia's way of life was unacceptable to Karuru, the elder of the local Indians. He did not like Urucuia, and to make matters worse, he strongly disapproved of teenagers developing feelings for one another.

Urucuia had two strikes against him, so he tried to be very discreet in his communication with Paloma. Of course, Lily wasn't helping in the area of keeping things quiet. The only way for them to communicate was through loving letters.

Even for someone as young as Lily, she quickly figured out why Urucuia had been stopping at the cashew tree so often. That was his hiding place for the letters.

The school year was almost over, and the children were taking their final exams. Paloma was busy studying and did not have time to answer Urucuia's love notes. After a couple of days without a response, Urucuia snuck away from his work at noon to leave a love note at the cashew tree. Apparently, someone saw him, for the next morning the noise of drums and voices could be heard in the valley. Indian Chief Karuru was declaring battle against Urucuia and his family. It was clear that he planned to punish Urucuia for his relationship with Paloma.

Indian Karuru was furious! He painted his body with the red juice of the Jenipapo fruit, and then added black stripes from the resin of some native plants. On his head he wore a colorful war bonnet made of parrot feathers and a skirt made of ostrich feathers. Necklaces of plant seeds and a bow and arrow finished his warrior outfit. He screamed and sang and danced to the beat of the drums as if he were in the old days before civilization.

Mr. Justo heard the confusion and noise and immediately saddled his mule and rode to the Indian village. Fortunately, he made it there just in time to stop Karuru from hurting anyone. "Karuru, stop! What are you doing?" Mr. Justo demanded.

"I can't stop, sir. This is a matter of honor and doing what is right. You don't know what is happening," Karuru shot back at him.

"No, I don't know what is happening. I just heard a bunch of commotion and came to investigate. Now, if you would just calm down and share with me what is happening, I'm sure we can figure out some sort of solution that doesn't involve the warpath. Believe me. There must be a better way to solve this problem as civilized people," Mr. Justo said.

"It depends on the kind of solution you propose, sir."

"So, tell me what is going on, Karuru."

"Urucuia betrayed our trust and has insulted our traditions. He wrote a letter to Paloma declaring his love and his plans to marry her in a civil ceremony. He then wants to move to the capital city."

"Where is the letter?" Mr. Justo asked.

"The young man left it beneath the cashew tree."

"Did you read the letter?"

"No, Mr. Justo. I cannot read. But a young man informed me of his intentions."

"Where is the letter now?"

"It is still beneath the cashew tree as proof to all who read it that Urucuia has dishonored our people."

"OK, let's all go to the cashew tree. I want to read the letter myself," Mr. Justo said.

Always the judge, Mr. Justo knew how to handle difficult situations and ask the right questions. Karuru settled down a bit while talking to Mr. Justo, and he left his weapons at home as he, Mr. Justo, and a group of curious men and women made their way up the hill from the village to the farm. There, beneath the cashew tree they found the letter hidden under a stone.

Mr. Justo began reading aloud; then he paused

"Wait a minute! This letter does not talk about marriage and running away to the capital city. Listen to what is written:

Sabia made a little hole in the cage
And flew, flew, flew, flew away
The girl who loved the pet so dear
Wept, wept, wept, wept all night

Sabia flew into the woods
To nest in a tall, tall tree
But the girl wanted the bird
"Come back, Sabia, my love"
The girl was sad, and she cried
"Sabia, I'm waiting for you"
From the treetop Sabia responded
"Don't cry, I'll be back, my love"

The poem was so funny that everyone laughed. What everyone didn't know is that Lily had written the poem. She had taken the love letter and left her poem in its place before all the commotion began, but it was a good thing that she had done so, for it defused a potentially dangerous situation.

Indian Karuru was ashamed and speechless. The young man who had spread the rumor about the two getting married was astonished and did not know what to say.

"Ladies and gentlemen, please return to your homes and work. There is no proof of the claim that Urucuia and Paloma are getting married. I will speak with Urucuia and Paloma as soon as possible."

Mr. Justo planned to talk to the teenagers as soon as possible. Maybe they were in love, or maybe they were just friends. Whatever the case may be, at the moment the most important thing had been to stop Karuru from going to war with Urucuia's family. Mr. Justo would get to the bottom of the subject as soon as possible. But unlike Karuru, he did not believe that falling in love was a crime.

Chapter 8

    School was out for the holidays, and with less to do on the farm, Mother and the children decided to visit some friends in the village and attend a wedding celebration that Mr. Justo was performing. The activities of the day flew by with much laugher and entertainment. After the wedding, Mother and the children enjoyed a leisurely stroll along the gravel road leading from the village to the farm. The children ran in all directions, laughing, singing, picking flowers, and collecting stones.

    A few days later Father returned home from a trip to the capital city. Squeals echoed throughout the house as the girls unpacked the Christmas decorations and gifts Father had brought with him. There were imported nuts, dried fruits, and European cheeses to savor. The treats were wonderful, but Christmas dinner would not be complete without a turkey from the farm. Lily was grateful for all the special treats and good food they would enjoy that holiday season. As Father always said, they were blessed and had much to be thankful for.

    During the holiday break, the family enjoyed a more leisurely way of life. After dinner they would lounge on the porch—Father would recline in his the hammock, Mother would rest in a comfortable canvas chair, and the kids would sprawl out on mats woven from leaves.

    Sometimes Mother told them stories, other times a neighbor joined the family for a visit, and then there were the evenings where they simply sat on the porch staring into the starry sky. Every once in a while they would hear the melancholy tune of an accordion float on the breeze from the valley below. In response to the tune, a nightingale often added his voice to the entertainment of the evening.

Lily loved the feel of the gentle breeze upon her skin. She also loved gazing at the starry sky with its beautiful moon and the different clusters of stars that formed pictures before Lily's eyes. One night Lily tried to count the stars. She tried to count each star as it showed up in the sky, but she soon lost track because there were so many. The sky seemed so close to her that she felt as if she could reach out and grab one of the stars in the palm of her hand.

It was calming to stare at the sky while surrounded by the people she loves. In her contentment, Lily often fell sound asleep.

One night while the family was enjoying a quiet evening on the porch, the teacher of the farm school came to announce her resignation. Her daughter had given birth to triplets, and she needed to go help her daughter with her expanding family. Mr. Justo and the children were happy for their teacher that she could go be with her daughter and grandchildren, but they were sad, too, because they were losing a good teacher.

Another evening Paloma and Urucuia showed up on the porch and announced that they were getting married and moving to the capital city. The family jumped up and embraced the couple. Everyone excitedly chattered at the same time, asking questions about the upcoming festivities. The couple asked Mr. Justo to be the judge for their wedding. They also asked if they could be married at the farm, and if Nydia would be the witness. Urucuia and Paloma's parents came with them to give permission for them to marry. Mr. Justo was pleased to see that Karuru had changed his opinion about the young couple and was no longer fighting them being together.

It was a time of change, but the biggest change was still to come. One evening Mr. Justo gathered the children in the living room and announced that the family was moving from the farm to a nearby town. It was his dream to give his children the opportunity to have a good education and be better prepared to face the future.

It was a huge surprise to the kids. Moving to the city and attending a bigger school sounded exciting. Nydia was happy, because she was moving to the city where she grew up, and now she could be closer to friends and family members.

The small city had two schools, one for the younger children and one for the older children. Marie and Meg were in the sixth and seventh grades, and they would be attending a private school. Leah, the oldest, preferred to obtain a degree in dressmaking; she was glad for the opportunity to live in a place where she could get a degree. Each of the children had a different objective in moving to the city. Marie wanted to find a handsome husband; Meg wanted to become a teacher; Tony wanted to find a job and make lots of money; while Tina and Felipe were satisfied with anything. Everyone was excited about the plans for the future—everyone except Lily.

During the last days of that special summer, Mother and the children spent their days packing and discussing all the details of their new home. They visited with friends and prepared to say their official farewell to the farm that they loved.

The scheduled moving day occurred on a dull, grey morning at the beginning of fall. Lily was not interesting in facts, schedules, agendas, or calendar. A big, noisy truck drove up the hill and parked beside the greenhouse. Friends and employees began the loading process, carrying boxes, luggage, and furniture to the waiting truck.

Lily was sad. Everything she had even known was about to change. Life would never be the same again. She saw tears in Meg's eyes, a deep sob choked Leah's voice, and tears rolled down Marie's cheeks. Father dabbed his face, trying to hide his own sadness as to leaving the farm. Mother looked out across the valley to the hills, then she checked the house once more to make sure they had all their belongings.

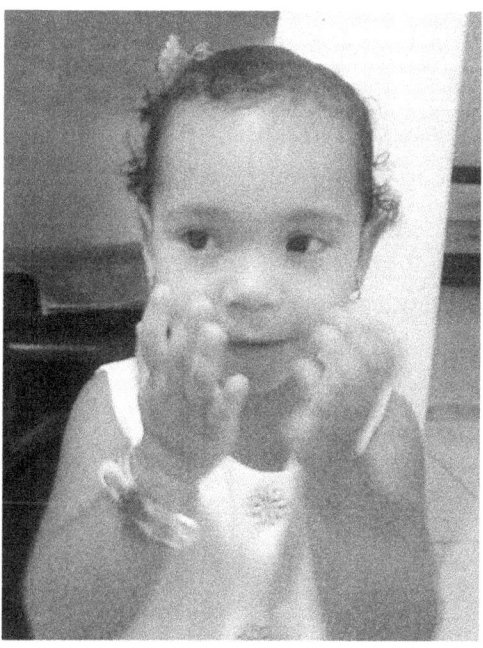

The family was ready to depart, when Father looked around and asked, "Where is Lily?"

"She is beneath the cashew tree," Felipe said.

Father walked across the yard to the cashew tree and sat down next to Lily.

"The cashew tree looks sad, Father. Who will play under it and love and care for it with us gone?" Lily asked. "It seems like it is exhaling. Listen to the wind, Father. It is moving the branches and rustling the leaves of the tree."

"Lily, the cashew tree will always be here. You can come and visit it and climb on its brunches again. Besides, I will be coming back to the farm frequently to take care of business. I will take care of the cashew tree for you."

"I know this is hard for you, but we need to go. This will not be the last time you see the farm. It's just that we won't be living in this house any longer."

Lily took Father's hand and walked toward the truck. As usual, Joey followed close behind Lily. She would miss her donkey so much. Almost as much as the cashew tree.

Lily took one final look at the farm, making a mental picture of where everything was and all her favorite things, including Zeze the rooster, who flew to the top of the highest fencepost and sang once more for Lily.

All of their friends hugged them and cried as they said goodbye. Then everyone climbed into the truck and drove down the hill toward the gravel road that would take them to their new home. The girls looked out the window until the farm slipped from their view. It was so hard for the girls to say goodbye to the people and things that were important to them, but the opportunities for a good education and a career helped the older children to accept the changes that were happening. Lily was still young and didn't understand everything, but she tried to make the most of it.

Chapter 9

The city was a small city, but it had a lot of conveniences that Lily was not used to seeing. There were two doctors and two pharmacies in the city, a church, a park, a small grocery store, and a movie theater that showed the same movie for months at a time before getting a new one.

One of the most exciting things about moving to the city was that Lily could now attend school. On the first day of school, the teacher tested Lily's reading level and assigned her to the first grade. Lily was a bubbly, talkative girl, and she quickly made friends with the other children. She loved telling her classmates stories about her adventures on the farm. Before long she earned the title of "best storyteller ever." At recess the kids would gather around Lily and listen to her tell made-up stories and real-life happenings, including stories about holiday celebrations, the farm animals, the forest, and the general workings of the farm. They urged her to not leave out any detail. Lily enjoyed the attention and reveled in her new role as storyteller.

However, Lily's happy world had a dark spot on it. Cristina was a pretty blond classmate who had been the most popular girl in the school until Lily came along. Before long, it became evident that Cristina was jealous of Lily. One day while Lily was telling stories to the other children, Cristina came over and said, "I hate stories! And I dislike farms, farm animals, and people who work on farms!"

"How can you hate farms? Your father is a farmer," Lily said.

"My father is not a farmer. He owns a very large farm. He is a businessman," Cristina shot back, with that she stomped off. A few days later the kids noticed that at recess Cristina walked to her home, which was right in front of the school, and spent the break playing inside.

"I wonder what Cristina says to her parents as to why she comes home each day," Lucy said.

"As long as she does not bother us or disrupt our storytelling time, I don't care," Lily said.

The next morning the teacher introduced a new first grade student to the class. Isabel came from a southern town and would be staying with her grandmother for a few months while her mother was recovering from surgery. The teacher sat Isabel beside Lily on the third row, and the two little girls immediately bonded. It was friendship at first sight. The girls were the same age, the same height and weight, and both loved telling stories.

Everyone got along well and enjoyed playing together and telling stories, except Cristina. One day during recess while the kids were swinging and playing, Cristina came over to where Isabel was swinging and, without saying a word, pushed her off the swing. As soon as the deed was done, Cristina ran to the classroom and sat at her desk as if nothing had happened. Isabel screamed as soon as she hit the gravel.

Lily and her classmates immediately ran to Isabel and helped her to her feet. As they looked at her injuries, they yelled for their teacher to come help them. Their teacher came running at the sound of the children yelling. She helped Isabel into the classroom, cleaned the wound, applied first aid medication, and made sure nothing was broken.

But even after she was cleaned up, Isabel would not calm down. She continued crying and crying.

"Please, children, sit down. I want to know what happening."

The students remained silent. Isabel tried to say Cristina's name through her sobs, but she couldn't spit out her name.

"Can someone please tell me what happened? I want to know the truth," the teacher demanded.

"Cristina did it," a number of children said at the same time.

"Did what?" The teacher wanted more answers.

"Cristina pushed me off the swing," Isabel finally said.

"Did anyone else see this happen? Did you see, Pedro?"

"No, teacher. I was practicing wrestling with James."

"Wrestling? We will talk about that later. Lucy, can you tell the truth?"

"Why me, teacher? Isabel already told you."

At that moment the school principal entered the classroom and handed the teacher an accident report. He asked her to answer the questions clearly and write down an explanation of the incident on the playground.

The teacher was about to declare that Cristina was innocent, because Cristina was a good student, and the teacher was unaware of how she had been treating Lily and Isabel.

"Sir, it was a natural accident that happens on a daily basis," the teacher said.

"It was indeed an accident, but it was an intentional accident. If you, madam, are looking for the truth, I can tell you what happened. The truth is that Cristina pushed Isabel off the swing. I saw everything."

Cristina slid down in her chair. She was embarrassed that she had been caught. She tried to hide her face, but she jumped in surprise when she heard her mother's voice. "Cristina, take your backpack and go home. You are grounded!" Her mother had apparently seen what had happened, too.

The principal asked his assistant to fill out the accident report. He then gave a copy to Isabel along with a letter to her grandmother.

The following day all the students returned to school except Cristina and Isabel. No one was worried about Cristina, but everyone wondered how Isabel was doing.

Lucy sat next to Lily and whispered to her ear, "Let's visit Isabel today after class. I want to make sure she is OK."

"That's a great idea. Do you know where Isabel lives?" Lily asked.

"Out, Out …" Lucy groaned as Thiago pulled her ponytail.

"I heard your plans," he whispered.

"OK, you can come with us, but you can't say anything to anyone," Lucy said.

Although the girls had thought it would just be them, James and Pedro ended up joining them as well with the excuse that Pedro lived close to Isabel's house. The group bolted out of the classroom as soon as the bell rang. They couldn't be too late getting home. Every minute counted.

"This is Isabel's grandmother's house," Pedro said when they reached the outside of a little house.

Isabel's grandmother was a lovely lady, and she received them with a warm smile, invited them to come in, and took them to the backyard patio where Isabel was playing tea party with her dolls. Isabel's leg was still bruised, but she got very excited when she saw her friends.

"I know how my granddaughter feels. Cristina not only hurt her leg, but she also hurt Isabel's heart. I'm glad she has good friends such as yourselves at that school, but I think it is best to send Isabel to a private school until her father comes to take her home," the elderly woman said. "I will not stand for

bullying and watch my granddaughter get hurt, both physically and emotionally. She needs to be in a school where she is accepted for who she is."

The kids were sad when they heard this news. They wanted Isabel to return to school. They were also angry at Cristina for her treatment of Isabel. Cristina was jealous of Isabel and Lily's friendship and how the other children loved to hear their stories. Unfortunately, Cristina let her hatred toward Isabel and Lily grow until she took it out on her unsuspecting target—Isabel.

Anytime anyone takes out their frustrations on another person, one or both people will get hurt. And once the deed is done, it can never be taken back.

The children visited with Isabel a little while longer before saying goodbye and heading home. They all held fond memories of their time together, but a note of sadness marked their separation as they thought about the one little girl who had ruined everything with one single act of meanness.

Chapter 10

The next few years in the city brought about a variety of changes for Lily and her siblings, some good and some bad.

It didn't take long for Tony, the eldest sibling, to get a job at an ice cream shop in town. Unfortunately, he dropped out of school and soon got a different job working at a bar. He then met a girl older than him and began dating her. He rebelled against his parents' instructions and counsel, spending nights away from home. Father and Mother discussed moving back to the farm to correct Tony's troubled ways, but the rest of the children were doing well in their studies.

Leah enrolled in a dressmaking course and finished the technical course in record time. While studying she got engaged to a fine gentleman and the family began making plans for an October wedding while the kids were on a vacation from school.

The wedding took place back at the farm with Mr. Justo officiating. It was a wonderful celebration that was attended by many friends and family. Leah was a beautiful bride and was so happy.

Of course, Leah wasn't the only one who was happy. Lily was so glad to be back on the farm for a visit. She climbed the cashew tree, rode Joey the donkey, and played with Joey's family, a gorgeous Jennet baby donkey.

All too soon vacation was over and the family returned to the city so the children could begin school. Everyone settled into their school routine within a few weeks, and then Father announced that he had to leave once again on a business trip. This was not an unusual occurrence, but everyone hated to see Father leave again. Before his departure, he gave Mother money for their regular household needs and a little extra in case of an emergency.

Mother put the money in a safe place and told the children to keep their friends away from that area of the house. Unfortunately, one day when Mother needed the money, she couldn't find it in her hiding place. She waited for the girls to return home from school, thinking that one of them may have moved the money to another location. But when the girls came home each of them promised her that they had not touched the money.

Mother was very frustrated and devastated. How was she to explain to Father the mysterious disappearance of the money. As she thought about who else could have took the money, she suspected Tony of the crime. Tony was making bad choices and staying out at night to party with his girlfriend. *Maybe he stole the money*, Mother thought. She waited up late that night and confronted him when he got home. Tony swore that he did not know about the money and begged her to trust him, but Mother would not listen. She suspected him over her daughters because of his poor lifestyle choices. Sadly, Tony was innocent, but Mother didn't want to believe it. That night after their conversation Tony left home to go live in the streets.

When Father returned home for the weekend, he was greeted with the bad news that the money was missing and that Tony had left home. Father believed deep in his heart that Tony was didn't take the money, but he couldn't prove it. The next week Father had to leave again. Once more he left money with her, this time instructing her to watch the girls carefully and investigate things at school if necessary.

Within a few days the money disappeared again. The next morning Mother observed that Meg didn't eat any breakfast and her purse looked stuffed. As Meg left the house to walk to school with some of her friends, Mother followed her at a safe distance to see what she would do. Upon arriving at school, Meg gave a gift to her teacher and offered snacks to her friends.

Mother had seen enough. She returned home and waited for Meg. When Meg came home from school that day, Mother got straight to the point.

"I saw you handing out gifts and snacks at school today. Where did you get the money to purchase such things."

Meg hung her head in shame. "I'm sorry, Mother. I just didn't know how to handle the situation. Some of the kids have been bullying me at school, so I thought if I bought them treats, they would stop teasing me and picking on me."

"Why didn't you tell me about the problem?" Mother asked.

"I don't know. I just figured I could solve things on my own by using the money to buy their friendship," Meg confessed.

"My dear, you can never buy someone's friendship. And even if you could, you stole from your family to make your situation better at school. That was certainly wrong!" Mother said. "Now that I know what has been happening, I will go to school and address the situation with the teacher."

"Oh, Mother, you can't do that. The teacher knows what is going on, but won't do anything about it. That is why I took a gift to the teacher as well."

"Then I will talk to the principal. This cannot keep going on," Mother stated. "I will wait until your father returns to determine your punishment for stealing. You know better! Your father is a judge. You know that people go to jail for stealing. You know that it is wrong! If you had come to us, we could have addressed this issue with the principal without you taking matters into your own hands."

Mother felt horrible that she had falsely accused Tony of stealing. The next time she saw him she apologized for mistrusting him. Tony forgave his mother, but he was disconnected from the family. To make matters worse, anytime Tony would come home for a visit Meg would try to stir up trouble.

Tony got so tired of his sister's tactics that he decided to leave town. Somehow someone found out about his plans and told Nydia. Upon hearing the news, she grabbed Lily and headed for the bus station.

"Lily, quick! We must go to the bus station and stop Tony from running away," Mother yelled.

Lily ran with her mother through the streets until they reached the bus station. When they reached the station, Mother described Tony to the ticket clerk and asked which bus he was on. The ticket clerk told her, and Mother and Lily ran to the bus, which had just closed its door and was backing out.

Mother wildly waved her arms and yelled for the bus driver to stop. Fortunately, the man saw her and stopped the bus and opened the door.

"What is the problem, lady?" he asked.

"My son is on this bus, and he is running away from home. He is under eighteen, and I want to talk to him."

The bus driver let Mother and Lily on the bus, and with tears in her eyes, Lily asked Tony to come home. "Please, Tony, please come home. Don't run away. I love you."

Tony was touched by the request of his youngest sister, and he agreed to return home. However, he didn't stay forever. Once he turned eighteen, Tony left home, and he didn't return for seven years.

Chapter 11

The years flew by, and the children continued their education at the school. After completing her third year at school, Lily was approved with honors to move up to the fourth grade. She could barely contain her excitement at being awarded honors for her work in the third grade. She eagerly told her mother and siblings, but she relished the thought of telling her father.

Every Friday morning he would arrive home by bus after a long week of working at the farm or at his legal office. From the walkway of their home in the city, Lily could see the bus station. She couldn't wait to share the good news with her father, so she sat on the walkway and waited until she saw the bus pull into the station. Then she ran as fast as her legs would carry her.

The meeting of father and daughter was sweet. She ran and threw her arms around Father, hugging him with all her might. As soon as she let go, she blurted out her good news.

"That's wonderful news, Lily. I'm so proud of you!" Father said. "But, Lily, you are almost a young lady now. You shouldn't be running through the streets like that."

"I don't care, Father. I just couldn't wait to see you," Lily said. "Here, let me carry your briefcase."

He gave her another hug and then they turned and walked toward home. As they walked, Lily filled him in on the news of the week at home and school. Father patiently listened to each word, smiling softly at her silly stories and serious comments.

Mother was expecting Father and had a delicious meal prepared for him. After he ate, Father took a warm bath and rested in his bedroom for the remainder of the day and all day Saturday. On Saturday night Father enjoyed reading the newspaper or a good magazine. That night he read the newspaper, which contained an article predicting a drought that would certainly affect the cocoa crop. Father and Mother discussed the news of the projected drought. It was a cause of concern, for they were still recovering from the wedding expenses and the birth of their eighth child, a baby boy.

"Do you think the newspaper is right?" Mother asked.

"Maybe; they are right most of the time. It has not rained for almost two months, and the temperature keeps rising and the color of the vegetation is beginning to change."

"If a drought happens, are we prepared?" Mother anxiously asked.

"I believe the newspaper is correct in their prediction. And I do not know what more we can do to cut costs and survive. Why don't we discuss this with the kids and see if they have any ideas how to save money?"

"Maybe we could go to the farm for few months," Mother suggested.

"I don't know. At this point and time moving to the farm will cost us quite a bit of money," Father said.

Mother and Father got quiet. Each was lost in his and her owns thoughts. For now, there was nothing more to say. They could discuss the matter tomorrow.

After breakfast the next morning the family gathered together to create a plan for how to financially survive the drought.

"We need to come up with something that is easy and profitable. The fruits and vegetables from the farm are enough to feed us and our employees. But we need to bring in money. One resource we do have left is the cassava," Father said. "We have plenty of it planted near the edge of the waterfall."

"Wonderful! I have an idea," Mother said. "We could make puba from the cassava roots and sell it here in the city."

"That is a great suggestion!" Father said. "I will send the cassava to you from the farm, and you and the girls can work to make the puba, and then together we can find a way to sell it."

Father returned to the farm the next day in much better spirits. The family had a plan of how to earn some money.

The cassava arrived two weeks later, and Mother and the girls set to work preparing the final product. One week later they had a large quantity of puba to be sold, but Meg and Tina, the oldest children still at home, did not want to sell the puba.

"No, Mother, please. We can't sell this puba in the streets. What will our friends say?" Meg and Tina whined.

"Well, somebody has to do it," Mother said. "You are the oldest, and you can take responsibility to help out where needed."

Tina obeyed her mother and went out in the streets to sell the puba. She managed pretty well, but she soon came back home, claiming that the heat was too much for her to bear. Mother needed to do something quick because the puba was only fresh for about five days. If they didn't sell what they had made, all of their hard work would be a waste.

Another Lily was younger, Mother didn't know who else to turn to, so she asked Lily to help her sell the puba. "OK, Mother. I can sell all of the puba. I know a lot of people in this city, and I assure you that I will sell everything today!"

With the faith of a child, for that is what she was, Lily took a large aluminum container, filled it with puba, and, with the help of her siblings, put the container on top of her head. She then went door to door, starting with her playmates' and classmates' parents, selling the product. A few hours later she returned with an empty container and a pocket full of money. She then filled up the container once more and headed back out. She planned to continue as long as the family needed the money. With Lily's success, Mother and the girls made more puba for her to sell.

One day while Lily was delivering the product to a restaurant she heard a gentleman ask the cashier if he knew of any houses for rent. He needed a house for a family of nine.

"Nine people? Do you need a house or a hotel?" the cashier asked.

"I need to rent a house for me, my wife, and our seven children."

"I'm sorry but I can't help you. I don't know of any houses for rent."

Lily recalled that their neighbor had his house for sale. Maybe he would be willing to rent it.

"Sir, I know of a house for sale in my neighborhood, but the owner may be willing to rent it. If you will go the bakery near the bus station, you can ask the owner about his home."

The man thanked her and left the restaurant. Lily forgot about the encounter until a few weeks later when a new family moved in next door. It was the same man who she had met at the restaurant.

"Mother, that is the man I told you about that I met at the restaurant. Where do you think they came from? Do you think they came from a farm as well?"

"I don't know, Lily. I wonder why they came to the city during this hard economic crisis."

"What crisis, Mother? We are making money every week selling puba, and Father continues sending us fruits and vegetables."

"We must not think just of ourselves. There are many people in need," Mother said.

While they were talking, the moving truck pulled away, leaving a few boxes on the walkway for the family to move inside. Mother headed outside to help their new neighbors with the last few boxes.

Lily and her siblings headed outside to play in the backyard, but they ended up staring through the fence at the five new neighborhood kids in their own backyard. The kids smiled at one another; it was friendship at first sight. Once all the boxes were inside, the new neighbor woman called to her children. "Kids, please come inside so that we can offer a prayer of thanksgiving to God for our new home."

"Mother, did you hear that?" Lily asked. "Our neighbor called her children in to have prayer."

"Yes, I heard, but I've never known someone who prays and thanks God for a move."

"When I went to the Baptist church, they never told me of such a prayer."

"I told you not to return to the Baptist church! There is a woman in the church who is our enemy," Mother said.

"Our enemy?" Lily said.

"Yes!" Mother said.

"But I don't understand, Mother."

"Your father and I have never told you this before, but when your father was very young, he married a woman who attends the Baptist church. She wanted to convert your father to her beliefs, and she forced him to do many things. They had children together, but they eventually separated. She and her children want the farm. They still cause problems for your father."

"What did Father do wrong? What makes this woman think she has any right to the farm?"

"The farm belongs to your father, and it will be yours someday."

"What is her name and the names of her children?" Lily asked.

"I don't know. Your father doesn't like to talk about it, so I don't ask. All I know is that he calls the one daughter 'girl.'"

"Girl! That's a strange name for a person!"

Marie and Meg were in the kitchen. They had been told about their father's previous marriage years before, and they had even met the ex-wife, "Girl," and some of the other half siblings. Girl practiced witchcraft and was a menace to her father. It seemed that she was intent on ruining his life and taking as much of his money as possible. She used to openly threaten Nydia and her children with her evil ways.

These were enough reasons for Mother to forbid her children to visit the Baptist church, for it seemed that the people who attended the church hated them and wanted to destroy them.

Chapter 12

Although the drought negatively impacted the local economy, Mr. Justo and his family survived those difficulties days very well. Although Mother did not believe in organized religion and that of a church, she and Father taught the children that there was a God in heaven who created the earth and who cared about His creation. Although some people thought the Justo family was just lucky when it came to surviving the drought, the family believed that it was because they worked hard, stuck together, and trusted in God's love that they weathered the storm.

The drought was in full swing. Each day the sun relentless beat down on the dry, cracked earth. In spite of the heat, the family prepared to celebrate another Christmas. Lily had heard that it got cold at Christmastime in the Northern Hemisphere, but in Brazil Christmas signaled summer vacation.

Lily and her siblings carefully set up the Nativity scene in the living room. The miniature figurines almost looked real. This year the children decided to make the scenery be as authentic as possible. They made a market place, palaces, houses, animals, shepherds and sheep, mountains, caves and a sandy desert to depict the town of Bethlehem. The kids could barely tolerate the heat as they worked together to assemble the Nativity. Mother knew the children needed a break, so she sent them to a river near their home to cool off in the water and to bring more sand home for their Nativity scene.

The kids cheered with the prospect of cooling off. As they got closer to the river, the temperature dropped slightly, and they could feel a slight breeze coming off the water. Everyone jumped in the water except for Marie and Meg who preferred to just get their feet wet.

Tina and Lily splashed in the refreshing water. Lily didn't know how to swim, but that didn't matter since the river was fairly shallow. As they waded in the river, they collected stones and watched the fish splash and dive around them. Suddenly a little red fish swam close to the girls and stuck its cute little face above the surface of the water. Then it dove down toward the bottom of the river, as if urging the girls to chase him.

Tina followed the fish, while Lily went in the opposite direction. There was a small island of sand that she wanted to explore down river a bit. The drought had significantly lowered the level of the water of the river. Once Lily reached the small island of sand, she discovered another small island parallel to it with a narrow canal running between them. The canal was about nine feet wide and twenty-four feet long, ending with a big rock at the right side of the canal. The water flowed a little more swiftly through the canal compared to the rest of the river, but Lily figured that she could manage. It didn't appear that deep, so she figured she could just wade across.

Lily began wading across the canal. As she reached the middle of the channel the bottom of the river seemed to disappear, and Lily was swept off her feet by the stronger current. Lily gasped for air as the river propelled her along. In a matter of seconds she reached the end of the canal and bumped into the rock that separated the two islands. She grabbed hold of the rock and tried to stand up, but the currents kept her down. Her head bobbed to the surface, and she took in a gulp of air and water before plunging beneath the surface again. All the while, she clawed at the rock, trying to find a handhold that would allow her to pull herself out of the water.

After the third time of coming up for air only to be pulled back down by the current, Lily thought it was hopeless and that she was going to drown. Lily was exhausted and didn't know how much longer she could hold on, but with her last bit of strength, she fought against the water, gulping in more air and water as she came to the surface. At that moment, a young man paddling a canoe saw her struggling and came to her rescue.

Marie, Meg, and Tina were getting ready to leave when they heard people shouting.

"A little girl has drowned!" said one woman.

"Is she alive? Does anyone know who this girl is?" asked another.

Marie, Meg, and Tina scanned the river for Lily, and when they didn't see her, they ran toward the crowd, hoping beyond hope that the little girl the people were talking about wasn't their dear sister.

The three sisters reached the circle of people surrounding the body of the little girl and pushed their way through until they could see the form of the child lying on the group. Tina gasped when she realized that it was Lily.

The girls, along with other bystanders, began doing CPR and rolling her over on her side to drain the water from her lungs and stomach. They continued to work diligently on Lily until she took a breath.

"She is alive!" everyone cried out in relief.

"She is breathing now," said one of the people who had helped Marie, Meg, and Tina resuscitate Lily. "She will be all right, but you need to get her home and put her to bed. She needs her rest."

A few people helped the sisters get Lily home, and then Mother and the girls took over her care. They got her out of her wet clothes and into bed, where she stayed for the next few days. The talk of the town was Lily's near-drowning experience and the miracle that had occurred to save her life.

For the rest of that week neighbors and friends visited Lily. In addition to seeing her, each person enjoyed looking at the Nativity the children had spent so much time constructing.

Lily felt very loved, and she took everyone's comments to heart: "It was a miracle." "It was the spirit of Christmas." "You are a brave little girl." "God's care and protection saved you."

There were many well-wishers, but Lily and Mother were most impressed by their new neighbor's visit. Mrs. Dulce brought some natural remedies with her to help Lily regain her strength and a little storybook about how God has a plan for each person.

Lily opened the book and read the title of the stories: "Noah's ark," "Angels protect little children," "God's plan for baby Moses," and many others.

"What kind of storybook is this?" Lily asked Mrs. Dulce.

"These stories tell us about God's plan for each person by sharing with us stories from the past. I like the one that talks about God protecting baby Moses. Oh, yes, and this other one: 'The Blazing Furnace.' Do you like the book, Lily?"

Lily nodded her head, and Mrs. Dulce continued talking. "Just as God protected Moses from the currents of the Nile River, He also protected and saved you from drowning. God sent His angels to rescue you. The Bible says in Psalm 34:7 that 'the angel of the Lord encamps around those who fear Him, and delivers them.' We are human, and we have to understand that life is fleeting in this world, but the Bible teaches us that God protects us and takes care of us according to His plan for our lives."

Mrs. Dulce took a breath and then asked Lily another question. "Have you heard the story of Daniel's three friends? The Bible tells the story of three men whose names were Mishael, Azariah, and Hananiah. The king of Babylon built a huge statue of himself and told all the people in the land that they were to worship the statue. The three Hebrew boys knew that God forbid the worship of anyone or anything other than God. The three young men refused to worship the statue, so the king condemned them to death in a fiery furnace. Before throwing them into the blazing fire, the king gave them one last chance to worship the statue and save themselves, but they said, 'If God wants to deliver us from the furnace of fire, He will deliver us, but if He does not want to, we still will not worship the statue.'"

Lily's eyes widened as she heard the story. Mrs. Dulce continued. "They trusted that God had a plan for their lives. When the king threw them into the furnace, Jesus appeared in the fire and delivered them from death, and the king was astonished and worshiped God because of it. Thus, they did not die, because God had a plan for their lives. Similarly, if God still has a plan for your life and my life here on this earth, we do not have to fear because nothing will happen to us until God completes His plan in our lives. And yet, if we follow God's plan and die in Him, we are assured of eternity and the best plan God has in the entire universe to take those who love Him to heaven to live forever."

Mrs. Dulce looked deep into Lily's eyes. "I am sure, Lily, that God has a wonderful plan for you and that you will soon discover it. I pray that your future can be in harmony to His magnificent will. I pray that you cheerfully trust Him and accept His wonderful plan for your life."

"Mrs. Dulce, where did you buy those storybooks?" Lily asked.

"I got them at my church bookstore. I have many others books. You are welcome to come to my home and select any book you may want to read."

"Mrs. Dulce, what church do you belong to?"

"I am a Seventh-day Adventist, and my husband and children are as well."

"So, you are a believer? Who are the Seventh-day Adventists? I have never heard about of that church before," interrupted Nydia.

"Yes, I am a believer in Jesus Christ. Seventh-day Adventists keep the commandments of God and maintain a firm faith in Jesus Christ. We are a large family of believers from around the world. When my husband was looking for a location to set up a mechanic shop, we also had the vision to preach the gospel and plant a Seventh-day Adventist Church here in this town. The Lord led us to this place."

"Excuse me if I am bothering you with our questions," Nydia said.

"No, you are not bothering me at all," Mrs. Dulce said.

Before leaving, Mrs. Dulce thanked her for being a good neighbor and invited Nydia to see her embroidery crafts. Both women loved embroidery and craftwork, and a great friendship was born that day.

Chapter 13

As soon as Lily felt better, Mrs. Dulce invited the family to vespers at her home. Nydia took Lily and the three youngest children with her. The family arrived at the house, and Mrs. Dulce warmly greeted them. As the family found seats, Mrs. Dulce turned to Lily and asked, "Would you help me with this box?"

"Yes, Lady Dulce. What is in the box?"

"There are Bibles in this box. Please give one Bible to each person here."

"Wow! This is fantastic! Look, Mother. Look at how many Bibles are in this box."

"Incredible!" Mother exclaimed. Turning to her neighbor, Nydia said, "Some years ago Lily and I set a goal of reading the Bible, but we didn't own one. I just can't believe it that you are giving us a Bible. I feel overwhelmed with joy."

"That is wonderful news, Nydia! See how the Lord is leading the way? He has provided a Bible for you and your family. Please take this Bible with you. I will be glad to help you understand what you read and answer any questions you might have about God's Word."

After the Bibles were passed out, Mrs. Dulce addressed the small group. "Remember how I told you that my husband and I wanted to start a Seventh-day Adventist Church is this city? Well, we rented a business suite by the bus station, and next Sabbath we will hold our first worship service at our new church. The vision for our church is to be part of the great commission that Jesus gave to His disciples to go into the world and preach the gospel, baptize people, and teach them the Word of God. We want to tell people about the life, death, and resurrection of Jesus Christ; the prophecies that point to the end of the world and Christ's second coming; and the wonderful plan of salvation and the saving power of God's love.

"The Holy Spirit will empower us to fill this city with the truths and knowledge of Jesus Christ. By faith, I can already see a large and strong church that will grow and thrive as we do our part to bring others to Jesus. Through the power of the Holy Spirit, many will be converted and saved."

God touched Nydia's heart, and once Mrs. Dulce was done speaking, she said, "I want to be a commissioner, too."

"Mother, can I be part of the great commission?" Lily asked. "I know many kids and adults, and I could invite all of them to learn about Jesus. Can I, Mother?"

A huge smile broke across Mrs. Dulce's face as she heard the sincerity in Nydia and Lily's voices. "Lily, you can most certainly be a missionary. The Lord will be pleased to have you and your mother working for Him." She put her arms around Nydia and Lily and whispered, "Salvation has come to your house. I look forward to studying the Bible with you and guiding you in your newfound journey with Jesus."

After the meeting, the family returned home and Nydia asked Lily to open the Bible and read the first passage she came to. Her heart burned within her to learn more about God's love. The little she knew, she already desired to follow God with all her heart and obey His commandments.

Over the next few days, Nydia devoured the Word of God. She took advantage of every chance Lily or Mrs. Dulce could read or talk to her about God. She desired God's mercy and forgiveness from the power of sin. Her conversion was sincere, clear, humble, and real. The more she studied, the more she changed. Her family and friends could testify to the transformation of her character, habits, manner of speech, and activities. She was one fire for Christ and desired to do His will. Jesus Christ was the center of her life. She constantly praised Jesus for the privilege to be chosen to receive the power of His pardon and to become a child of God. The love of God brought her peace, love, and happiness.

Nydia was so excited about her newfound faith, but she feared what Mr. Justo would think, for he did not support organized religion.

The next Sabbath Mrs. Dulce passed Lily on the sidewalk. "I missed you at church today, but don't forget that this afternoon at four o'clock we are having our first evangelistic training meeting so that we can learn how to be fishers' of men."

"I don't know if I can attend," Lily said. "But I want to."

"I will talk to your mother," Mrs. Dulce said.

"It is OK with me that Lily be active at church, but I am worried about what her father will say. He still doesn't know about our faith. He is home this weekend, but I have been waiting for the perfect moment to tell him."

"Why don't you let Lily ask him for permission to attend this afternoon's meeting? I believe in prayer, and I have been praying that your husband would accept your newfound faith. God can work everything out for you."

Later that afternoon Lily approached her father and told him everything that had happened after attending the meeting at Mrs. Dulce's house.

"A church that meets on Saturday? What church is this?"

Nydia stepped forward and together she and Lily explained the best they could about the Seventh-day Adventist Church and the fourth commandment of God's law. They were still babies in their faith, but they shared what they knew.

"I don't know a lot yet, but all that we have told you is in the Bible," Lily said. "God wants us to keep the Sabbath day."

"It is fine with me. You have my permission to attend this church. In fact, the whole family has my permission. What you have told me sounds very interesting," Father said.

Lily gave him a big hug and then went to get ready to attend the afternoon training meeting. She also eagerly looked forward to attending church the next Sabbath.

At church Lily and the others children received training in welcoming people and scheduling a Bible study with an adult. Soon another Adventist family moved to the city and joined the church. The new family, along with the evangelistic materials and resources that the conference sent, were a big help in moving the church forward in their efforts to share the gospel with their community.

The little church diligently planned for the upcoming evangelistic meetings. Finally, the date of the meetings arrived. Everyone was ready. The conference sent singers and a guest preacher. Lily was especially excited, for she had invited a lot of people. On the opening night Lily brought forty-two guests with her, and on the second and third evenings she brought forty-five guests.

The Holy Spirit blessed the work of the faithful members, and at the end of the meetings many souls gave their hearts to Christ. Within six months the church moved to a new building. It was small, but there was land next door that they could build a larger church on as more people joined and money became available.

Approximately one year after Lily and her mother first heard the gospel truth, Lily was baptized, along with about thirty other people. They were the first fruits of the evangelist meetings. The church continued growing in numbers, in love, and in zeal for God's Word.

Lily loved God, and she loved telling people about His love. She had a way of talking to people, and she was not bashful in inviting people to come to church. For these reasons, she joined the evangelism group from the church that held meetings around the city each Sunday. Rain or shine, day or night, traveling by foot or by bus, every Sunday the group headed out across the city to share the gospel with those they met.

Because of their efforts and God's blessings, the church grew. And after almost two years the church membership was well over one hundred members. Lily enjoyed the variety of preachers that spoke each Sabbath. One such preacher was a high school teacher who came to the city two or three days a week and stayed at the Dulce's home. For more than twenty years he had attended the Baptist church, but after learning about the fourth commandment, he joined the Seventh-day Adventist Church. Mr. Amastor was truly a disciple of Christ, and after getting to know him, Nydia thought that he was just the person to share the gospel with her husband.

Just as Jesus met Nicodemus in the evening in the garden, Mr. Amastor met Mr. Justo one evening at his home. After introducing himself and sharing a bit of information about himself, Mr. Amastor told Mr. Justo the story of Nicodemus, sharing that unless a person is born again, he or she cannot see the kingdom of God.

Mr. Justo was an intellectual man of great moral integrity, but he knew nothing about spiritual principles. Just as Nicodemus, Mr. Justo was a good man—a good father, good husband, and good friend—but he needed a new heart to discern spiritual things and he needed to be transformed by the grace of God. That evening Mr. Amastor shared with Mr. Justo the plan of salvation, the love of God through the sacrifice of Jesus Christ, the free gift of grace and forgiveness, and the promise of eternal life through the righteousness of Jesus.

Lily and Nydia had shared this with him before, but that evening it was as if a curtain was lifted from his head and heart, and he clearly saw the need of a Savior and Redeemer. With Mr. Amastor's guidance, Mr. Justo gave his heart to God and committed to follow Him for the rest of his life. Lily and Mother were ecstatic when they heard the joyous news of Father's conversion.

What they didn't know is that there was soon to be another event worthy of celebration. One day as Lily was standing in the front yard she saw a handsome young man walking toward him. As he drew closer, she recognized the man to be Tony. She was almost rendered speechless, but she managed to shout out, "Mother, Tony has come home. Tony is here!"

Mother could hardly believe her eyes, but in a matter of minutes Tony stood before her.

"Hello, Mother. Forgive me for taking so long to find my way back home," Tony said as he hugged his mother.

As they went inside, Lily offered up a silent prayer to God for His goodness. There was much to be thankful for and praise Him for.

Chapter 14

Father studied the Bible and embraced the truths that Lily and Mother had adopted a few years ago. Within a short timeframe he asked to be baptized and began studying to join the Seventh-day Adventist Church. It was around this time that he decided to take the family to the farm. He didn't say how long they would stay, but Mother figured they would be there for several months. Lily didn't argue about missing school—she didn't mind living on the farm again. In fact, she cherished the idea as she thought about all the memories of her childhood. Now that she had a baby sister, Leonor, she planned to show her all around the farm so that she, too, could have fond memories of this special place.

They had been living on the farm for about one month, when Father's birthday rolled around on January 7. A big celebration was planned for their beloved father. Leah and her family, Marie and her family, and the rest of the siblings came to the farm to help celebrate his birthday, but on the morning of the big day, Father was really sick and couldn't get up.

The celebration was postponed until Father felt up to celebrating. Instead of the planned activities, the family read Psalm 71 for worship. Everyone was sad that Father was sick and couldn't enjoy his birthday.

Three days later Father was worse, so Mother and Meg took him to the nearest hospital. The doctors examined him, ran a variety of tests, and gave him medicine. However, instead of getting better, Father grew worse. Another three days went by, and on January 13, the doctor told Mother the bad news that he didn't think Father would make it.

Mother called all the children to come see their father. Somehow Girl, one of the daughter's from Father's first marriage, also showed up. However, she treated Mother and the rest of the family with disrespect and contempt.

Very early the next morning Mr. Justo asked Nydia to have Lily and baby Leonor come to the hospital so that he could see them once more. He also requested that Mr. Amastor, his spiritual mentor, come to the hospital.

Lily and her baby sister arrived at the hospital around 3:30 in the afternoon just as Mr. Amastor was leaving. He and Mr. Justo had had a lovely conversation, and Mr. Justo reaffirmed his faith, trust, and hope in Jesus Christ.

Father's face resembled pure joy and peace when he saw his girls. Leonor jumped on the hospital bed and hugged and kissed her father. She then proceeded to recite the new words she had added to her vocabulary in the last week. It was a wonderful moment between Father and his youngest girls.

Lily and Leonor left the hospital around 5:00 p.m. and went to Marie's house, which was just a few miles away, to spend the night.

As soon they left the hospital, Girl showed up and demanded that she speak with her father alone. Nydia and Meg refused to leave the room, but Girl was adamant. With all the commotion, Father became anxious, and the medical equipment that he was connected to started beeping. The nurses rushed into the room, calmed him down, connected oxygen to his nostrils, and ordered that everyone talk calmly and politely or they would have to leave.

Girl promised to behave, but she insisted on talking to her father privately, so she sat by his bedside and whispered into his ear. She asked him something trivial and he answered her. Then he said, "I am thirsty." Girl immediately grabbed a paper cup, filled it with water, and poured some into his mouth without sitting him up first or allowing him to lightly sip from the cup. Nydia and Meg witnessed the whole scene as Father began to choke.

"Help! Help! Please help my husband. He is choking to death!" Nydia yelled into the hallway, trying to attract the attention of the nurses.

All at once nurses and doctors ran into the room, lifted his head up, and started CPR, but it was too late. It had only taken a few minutes, but he was gone.

Girl, still holding the paper cup in her hand, passively said, "I am sorry. He asked for some water."

"How could you?" Nydia yelled. "You killed him! You killed your father!"

The director of the hospital promised to investigate the case, but in the meantime he sent Nydia and Meg home. Mother shared the sad news with the children, and everyone cried and mourned for the father they loved and adored.

The next morning Nydia, her children, and other family members and friends gathered to mourn the loss of Mr. Justo and hold the funeral ceremony. Among the crowd of mourners, Lily saw a man whom she recognized from her past.

"I can't believe it! I know you! You are the intruder who I saw at the farm many years ago. Yes, you are the burglar, the thief, who tried to break into our house," Lily said. "I would recognize your face anywhere!"

Marie and Meg moved to put their arms around Lily and comfort her. They recognized the man as Caipora, Girl's brother and one of Father's children from his first marriage.

"What is she saying?" one of the guests asked.

"I don't know," another person said. "I think she is delusional. She has just lost her father and is obviously grief stricken."

Mother called Lily to come closer. The coffin was about to be sealed and moved to the cemetery for burial.

"Everything is happening so fast, Mother," Lily said. "I don't like it."

After the burial ceremony, Leah and Marie returned to their homes, and Mother, Meg, and the younger children returned to the farm, while Leonor kept asking, "Where is Daddy? Is he coming home later?"

Mother and Meg spent that night talking, crying, grieving, and analyzing the costs of hiring an attorney to represent them before a judge to determine their rights to the farm. At the funeral they had heard that Girl and her siblings had hired an attorney to represent them, for they wanted the farm for themselves. They faced difficult times ahead of them. Meg needed money to pay for her last two years at school, and they needed an attorney. Not to mention food and the monthly expenses of living. Mother had no idea where the money was going to come from.

Lily couldn't sleep either. She tossed and turned. Around midnight she opened the window in her room and looked out over the hills, the valley, the river, and the trees. The moon peeked from behind a cloud and illuminated the scene before her. All nature was silent, as if mourning with her the loss of a great man. The farm that she loved now seemed somehow empty and lonely without her father's presence.

As she stood there at the window, a light breeze began to blow, stirring the branches and causing the leaves to dance. In the midst of her sorrow and the stillness of the night, she knew life had to go on. Yet her heart felt as if it would stop. *God, how could you let this happen?* her heart cried out. *I don't know how to live life without my father.*

Lily stood there at the window, lost in her thoughts and questions and grief until the moon and stars disappeared and the faint tint of red and orange dawned on the horizon. The first rays of a new day shone through the window, pushing the darkness from the room and lighting the small table and Bible that Lily kept in her room. She felt the presence of God and His assurance that He would walk with her through the challenging days that lay before her.

Later that day friends came to the house to express their condolences. Others sent cards and messages of comfort. Among the many cards that arrived over the next few days, one was from the members of the Adventist Church.

> Dear Lily and Sister Nydia,
>
> The Bible says that our life is like a light. It also says that life is like a plant that is born, grows, bears fruit, and then goes back to the earth. God created us and gave us a body, soul, and spirit. But our bodies are only temporary; they degenerate over time. When the body returns to the ground, the soul and spirit return to God who gave it.
>
> The Bible promises that those who love God and trust in His Son, Jesus Christ, will live again. When Christ returns to this earth at the second coming, the dead in Christ will be resurrected and will be given a glorified body, a wonderful body that will never die.
>
> In 1 Thessalonians 4:13 the Bible says that we should not grieve for those who die in the hope of Jesus Christ, but we must comfort ourselves because we believe that one day those who died in Christ will be resurrected. At that glorious day we will all be reunited to live together with Jesus forever in heaven. Amen.
>
> Your sisters and brothers in Christ

Lily was thankful for the blessed home she and her family had. As

King David wrote in Psalm 43:5, she would put her hope in God and would praise Him in spite of the hurt she felt, for a better day was coming.

Chapter 15

A few friends remained loyal to the memory of Mr. Justo and supported Nydia and her children as they battled for possession of the farm. Shortly after the funeral, Girl and her siblings filed a lawsuit against Nydia and her children, claiming that the farm was theirs. Girl used every form of manipulation she could think of to cause the court to side with her. She even went so far as to try and alter the birth certificates of Nydia's children, who were Girl's half brothers and sisters. She also bribed people into telling lies about Nydia and the children in an effort to sway the court to side in her favor.

A week before the court hearing, Girl showed up at the farm and sprinkled a kind of powder and liquid around the house as part of her witchcraft practices. She threatened the children as they watched her walk around the house, calling them names and treating them with contempt.

As the storm raged around them, Mother and the children persevered in prayer, crying out to God for protection and deliverance from Girl and her evil tactics. Mother comforted them with a passage in Isaiah that talked about the fall of the king of Babylon and God's triumph over wickedness. She reminded them to trust in God. "If God is with us, who can be against us?" she asked. "We have nothing to fear or worry about with God on our side."

The appointed day of the court hearing came, and Girl showed up with an air of confidence around her. She was fully convinced of her victory. She trusted in her witchcraft, her attorney, and her influence in the town, but she forgot that Nydia served a powerful and loving God who was ready to act and intervene on behalf of His children.

That day Girl was defeated in her efforts to take the farm, and the judge made it clear that she could not appeal the decision. However, the judge did rule that the farm was to be equally shared. One of Girl's brothers was appointed manager of the farm, and all proceeds were to be divided so that Nydia and her children would be supported. The case was closed.

Girl was furious. She was not content with half. She wanted everything! However, the court had spoken, so she returned to her home in the capital city.

With the court case settled, life resumed. Meg moved to another city to finish her degree, the oldest children returned to their homes to continue their lives, and Mother and the youngest children returned to their small home in the city.

Sadly, just as Mother predicted, money from the profits of the farm lasted only a few months, and then Girl and her siblings rebelled against the court mandate and kept all the money for themselves.

Nydia had a small garden at the farm that she tended, and sometimes it produced enough food for the week, but other times there was only enough food for a few days. The travel to and from the farm was hard on Nydia, but it was the only assurance of food, as there was no place to farm in the city. Once in a while Meg would send money home from her job, and sometimes Leah would bring over a hot meal for Mother and the children.

Before long the electricity to the house was turned off, as was the water. For weeks Lily went to school hungry, for the only thing she had for breakfast was Kool-Aid. She was always hungry, and there didn't seem to be any way out of their dark situation. The winter nights seemed to last an eternity, and as Lily listened to every drop of water dripping from the corner of her room, she hoped that maybe Mother could bring some fruit or vegetables home to alleviate her hunger.

Lily knew how much her mother was sacrificing her health, traveling to and from the farm each week, waiting beside the road for a bus or a free ride from a kind individual. It was tiring, and her mother was not in good health.

One day as Nydia made the trek to the farm and back to the city a car stopped and a chubby, short, and half-bald man opened the door and said, "Where do you want to go?"

"I need to go home, sir. May I ride with you?"

"Yes, please climb in the car. Where is your home? And from where are you coming? This is a horrible day to be outside. It is so rainy and cold."

As they rode along, Nydia briefly shared her story with the stranger, but when she mentioned that she was Mr. Justo's widow, the man interrupted her.

"You are the widow of my great friend, Mr. Justo?" he asked.

"Yes, sir, I am. Who are you?"

Nydia was surprised to learn that he was one of the richest men in the region, although he had a reputation of being an outlaw and a man who accumulated his wealth at the expense of others. She couldn't imagine why her husband had been friends with Mr. Dualdo. However, she kept these thoughts to herself.

"I didn't know you were friends with my departed husband. How close were you?" she asked, trying to figure out the situation.

"Mr. Justo was a very wise man. He advised me on many occasions and was my moral mentor. He helped me many times when I was still very poor. Once I became wealthy, I tried to thank him or compensate for all the favors he had done for me, but he always told me that my friendship was enough. Maybe now is the right time for me to show my appreciation and help his family. Is there anything I could do for you and your children? I have heard of all the problems that Mr. Justo's first children are causing in the court system. If you agree, I am sure that I can help you."

Nydia was silent for a moment. She didn't know what to say or do, but then her thoughts turned to her hungry children and her deplorable state of health from the work of trying to keep food on the table. "What do you propose, Mr. Dualdo?" she finally asked.

"What if I buy the farm? That way you would have the inheritance money in hand and would be able to provide for your family here in the city," he suggested.

"Sir, that would be wonderful, for I have six children under the age of eighteen that I am responsible for providing for," she said. Leonor was the baby of the family, and before her birth, Mother and Father had had three boys. So there was four children younger than Lily who had a lot of schooling ahead of them.

"I'm sure you will want to talk to your children about this proposal. If you decided to proceed, I will have my attorneys take care of the legal process. For now, I would like you to stop by my farm and take two gallons of milk home with you for the children. Also, here is some money for groceries."

Mr. Dualdo was very courteous and very persuasive. He seemed genuine in his desire to help Nydia and her children in memory of his friendship with Mr. Justo. However, Nydia did wonder about the rumors of his reputation.

After giving her the milk and money for groceries, Mr. Dualdo's chauffeur took Nydia home. The kids burst out of the house at the sound of the car stopping in front of their house. And what a surprise awaited them as Mother emerged with milk and food to eat. Rony grabbed the jar of milk and screamed, "Guys, guess who is here?"

"My boboca is here," said JuJu, who liked to give sweet nicknames to his mother.

"Mommy is home," shouted Leonor.

All of the children joyfully gathered around Mother as she told them about her encounter with Mr. Dualdo. Then she poured them milk and gave them fruit to eat while she sent Lily to the store to buy food for lunch and dinner.

Mother discussed the proposal with the older children, and it was decided that it was in the best interest of the family to accept his offer. It would be better to have him own and operate the farm compared to Girl and her siblings. One week later Nydia went to Mr. Dualdo's farm and accepted the proposed sale and agreed upon the price and conditions of the purchase. It was agreed upon that Mr. Dualdo would pay a certain amount of money to each child up front, in addition to making small monthly payments to Nydia so that she could provide for her children.

All of the children came home for the sale of the farm. Tony lived in another state, but even he came home. And so, the Good Vision Farm was sold to Mr. Dualdo, and Nydia and the children turned the page on a sad chapter in their lives.

After the sale, Marie and her family moved to another state, and Meg returned to school to finish her degree in early childhood education. Mother dedicated her time to taking care of her children and getting involved in church activities, which was a bright spot in her life.

The church was growing strong and now had 120 members. Sadly, tragedy struck when Mrs. Dulce, the pioneer of the church, was diagnosed with a terminal disease and only given a few months to live. Her father's death was still fresh in her mind, and Lily hated the thought of saying goodbye to another person she loved. However, Mrs. Dulce was the picture of peace. She placed her trust in Jesus and the hope of His second coming, and when she died, she went to sleep with the promise of seeing her family and friends once again in heaven.

Lily can't wait to meet Mrs. Dulce in heaven and tell her that after her death the church continued to grow until it reached 400 members and started nine other daughter churches in the city and about six other daughter churches in the surrounding cities.

Chapter 16

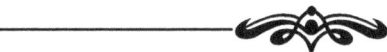

Nydia trusted Mr. Dualdo and his attorney with everything. She signed paperwork selling the farm, and Mr. Dualdo gave her the agreed upon money for the sale. Nydia felt that everything was handled professionally and legally. However, as soon as Girl found out about the situation, she filed a motion with the court requesting that the sale be considered null and void because a judge was not consulted regarding the right to sell or not sell.

Mr. Dualdo and his attorneys responded to the claim, and after a few days Girl and Mr. Dualdo received a court notification stating that the whole process of buying or selling the Good Vision Farm was on hold until further notice.

Mr. Dualdo remained calm throughout the whole process. He knew that Nydia was not able of return the money he already gave her or her children. He decided to wait patiently for the court authorization, which he believed would come in time.

The years passed quickly, and before she knew it Lily was a high school senior. While looking for work at the high school she was attending, Lily met a teacher who was also an attorney. As Lily got to know him, she shared the whole story of the farm inheritance with him, and he kindly offered to help in any way he could.

Mr. Lamb asked her lots of questions, and then he set about verifying all the details. A few months later he met with Nydia and asked additional questions and obtained other documents that he felt would help to resolve the problem.

Through the unexpected kindness of Mr. Lamb, God once more blessed their family and helped them along their way. Mr. Lamb faithfully worked for two years on the case until everything was resolved. Lily could not be present for the final resolution, for she was away at college, but she maintained contact with Mr. Lamb and thanked him again and again for his tireless work on their behalf.

Lily sent the following note to Mr. Lamb: "You acted as an agent of God and brought hope and help to my family without fearing the challenges or hostility that may have fallen on you. You have worked on behalf of my family and have restored our dignity, respect, and honor to my father's memory. I will thank God for you every time your name crosses my mind."

Thanks to Mr. Lamb's work, the court ruled that Nydia and her children still owned the farm along with Girl and her siblings. They ruled that Mr. Dualdo had not followed the appropriate legal channels to purchase the farm. The two groups of half siblings still did not like one another, but they were all adults now, except for two of Nydia's children, so they agreed to work together on the upcoming cacao harvest.

Then one morning Mr. Dualdo unexpected came on to the property with men and guns and demanded that he owned the farm and that he deserved to harvest the cacao.

Felipe refused to stand by and watch all of their hard work go to waste, so he bravely stood up to Mr. Dualdo and informed him that the court had made its ruling. Mr. Dualdo was furious. He grabbed Felipe and tied him to a mango tree beside the house and ordered his men to shoot him. Everyone stood still. What was supposed to be a peaceful takeover by showing their brute force was turning heated, and many of Mr. Dualdo's men didn't want the blood of an innocent young man on their hands or be charged with murder.

Fortunately, Mr. Dualdo changed his mind and decided to leave Felipe tied up instead of shooting him. He then ordered his men to fill the trucks with as much cacao as possible and take the crop back to his warehouse. The men set to work.

Meanwhile, one of the young men ran to the closest town to alert the sheriff as to the problem. Mr. Dualdo and his men were just pulling out onto the highway from the farm road when the sheriff stopped them.

"What do you think you are doing with all of those cacao beans?" the sheriff asked. "This isn't your property. I order you to return those beans."

"This is my rightful property, and you can't tell me what to do," Mr. Dualdo said.

Mr. Dualdo had outsmarted the law before, and he figured he could do so again. He disregarded the sheriff's command and drove the thirty miles to his home.

Later that evening he received notification from the sheriff that he was to come to the police station the next day or be arrested. In addition, they presented him with legal notifications from the Federal Revenue Treasury and a number of financial institutions accusing him of a variety of crimes.

The strong and courageous Mr. Dualdo could not resist this time. The law appeared to have caught up with him. It was too much to him. That evening his blood pressure skyrocketed, and he suffered a heart attack. His family took him to the hospital, but he passed away that night.

Everyone expected that one of Mr. Dualdo's heirs would continue the fight for the farm, but no one did. Instead, the family was once again left to sort out their differences about the farm. However, now that everyone was older, the children on both sides fought more with each other and amongst themselves.

In the midst of all this, Girl lost two of her sons. One was murdered and another one died after an extended illness. With the loss of her children, some of the fire seemed to go out of Girl, and she did not fit so hard to keep the farm.

After much negotiations and discussion, both sides agreed to sell the farm. They entertained a few offers, but in the end one of Mr. Dualdo's heirs purchased the farm. This time the sale followed the legal process and was approved by the court.

All of the siblings on both sides received an equal portion of the sale, and each took it as an opportunity to start a new life.

Lily was in the United States at the time of the settlement, but she was struggling to find permanent employment and was disenchanted with her circumstances, so she returned home to her mother.

Chapter 17

Lily's dream of owning the farm and operating it herself seemed to be a thing of the past now that it was sold. No matter how much that was her desire, the fact of the matter was that she had very little money.

Lily loved her mother, but after a time of being back home, she felt that she must go to the capital city and find a job. Nydia could not hold her daughter much longer; after all, Lily was a young adult. She was a devoted and obedient child to the Lord and to her mother. Mother sent Lily on her way with her blessing.

Once she arrived in the capital city, Lily found enough odd jobs to pay for a room and food. However, she did not earn enough to pay for bus far, so she had to walk miles each day to get to her jobs.

One day while she was walking through a fancy residential neighborhood, she noticed two gentlemen talking in English. She thought that they looked like evangelistic missionaries, so Lily approached them and introduced herself. The three of them struck up a conversation and talked about a wide variety of topics, including the Bible. Before parting they invited her to worship with them in an English-speaking church. Lily thanked them for the offer and then headed on her way. She did not have a church family in the capital city, and she longed to worship and interact with other believers. However, it was a non-denominational church that worshipped on Sunday instead of the Sabbath day. Weeks went by, and she finally decided to attend the church one Sunday, where she met the two men she had seen in the street.

The three once again struck up a conversation. Then, before she knew it, they were offering her a job.

"You could be so helpful to us, Lily. We just need someone to translate our sermons and go with us on home visits to translate our conversations."

"I don't know. My English isn't that good. I've only taken one second-language course. My skills are limited to that and what I have picked up through popular conversation."

"That is just what we need. Besides, your knowledge of the Bible is wonderful, and that is what matters most. In exchange for your work, we can offer you room and board. You would work about two weeks each month."

"But I am a Seventh-day Adventist. I believe in attending church on Saturday in accordance to the fourth commandment," Lily stated, thinking that this would end the conversation.

"We don't care. We just know that you love the Lord and sharing the good news of Jesus Christ with others. This is exactly what we came to do in Brazil. Please, will you be our translator? You do not have to say anything that goes against the Bible."

Lily accepted the position as translator, and over the next eight months, she welcomed seven groups of missionaries and trained and worked with them. They were impressed with her work and constantly praised God for the results of their evangelistic efforts. They were so satisfied with Lily's work that they invited her to visit the United States and stay with them as long as she wanted.

This was an opportunity of a lifetime to return to the United States. Lily began saving her money for the trip. But before she could go, she needed a visa, which often took quite some time. Lily took her passport and a letter from the missionaries inviting her to the United States to the U.S. Embassy. And within twenty minutes she walked out with her visa—it was a miracle.

After everything was arranged, Lily called Mother and told her the news.

"No, Lily, please don't go back to the United States! Try to find a job here in your hometown," Mother pleaded.

"I know your feelings, Mother. I know how much you love me, and I love you too, but I need to find a better paying job. I need a job where I can earn enough money to buy back the farm. I need a job where I can make a career of it and secure my retirement. I don't feel like I can do that here."

"What are you talking about, Lily? Don't you remember the first time you went to the States with big dreams and aspirations of making lots of money. However, you returned home penniless! Also, I fear for your spiritual growth and your journey with God. You are not keeping His holy commandments now that you are working for that church. I also fear that you may get involved in the struggle to accumulate money and fall into temptations and evil deceptions because of a love of money."

"Mother, I promise you that I will never turn my back on God, my Savior! I just want to work hard and come back home with extra money in my wallet for my family and me. I plan to continue working for the Lord. In fact, it is my desire to find an Adventist Church in the States and be able to bring back resources to Brazil for our brothers and sisters who are in need," Lily said.

"You are correct that I am still hurt and disappointed from my first trip to the States. It certainly didn't go as I had planned, but I feel that God is calling me to try again. I want to overcome the difficulties and let God build my character. The language translation I did for the English-speaking church I want to do for our Adventist Church. I want to continue to spread the gospel and tell people about the three angels' messages. I am firm in my desire to serve the Lord. Furthermore, Mother, I feel a strong sense of responsibility to preserve the legacy of my father, not only to get an education, but to once again operate his farm, the Good Vision Farm, our farm."

Lily continued, "If I am going to purchase the farm, I need to get a better paying job. I am confident that with Jesus' guidance I will succeed. I will not give attention to my limitations; I will not be frustrated for the wrongs that will happen to me; I will wrestle the evil things under my feet, as it is written in Psalm 91, for I know in whom I have believed."

"I can see that you are determined to continue your journey and fulfill your dreams and goals," Mother said. "Everything is possible with God. However, I want you to remember that material wealth is not our priority. The peace of Jesus Christ is the only thing that can give you satisfaction in this life. It is my desire that you focus on Jesus and look to Him for all wisdom and guidance. Follow Him at all times. I will miss you and will think about you at all times. Go in peace, but come back soon."

Chapter 18

Words have power. Words can change one for the better. Lily found stability to continue her journey with her mother's blessing. With everything in place, Lily set a date for her flight to the States and sent a message to Pastor Roy with her flight information so that he could pick her up.

Christmas was just around the corner when Lily arrived in the States. The streets, stores, homes, and churches were all beautifully decorated for Christmas. Lily gladly joined in the festivities.

Lily stayed with Pastor Roy and his family for a few months, and then he introduced her to the regional president of the Baptist conference. He offered her a secretarial job and help with securing her legal immigration paperwork. Lily was amazed at the outpouring of support, but her conscience bothered her that she would be working for a church that didn't follow the Bible.

She knew that God could open up another opportunity if she stayed true to her beliefs. She decided it was more important for her not to compromise her beliefs than to secure a good job. Lily decided to turn the job down and move to another state, trusting that God would open the right door for her.

While she was trying to find a place to live and a job in her new surroundings, she received a shocking call from home. JuJu had been in a car accident and had died two hours after the crash. It was tremendous shock to everyone in the family, yet they clung to God's promises that all things work together for good to those who love God. It was later discovered that while the doctors and nurses worked on JuJu at the hospital he shared with them his faith in Jesus and the assurance of salvation that he possessed. When he took his last breath, he was at peace with his Creator. Some of the doctors and nurses had never heard about God and His love, yet they heard about Him from the lips of a young man who was dying.

The family found strength in this news and JuJu's faithfulness to God. But this made them long even more for Christ's coming when they would be reunited with Father and JuJu.

Lily wanted to come home, but Mother insisted that there was no need for her to spend the money to return. Lily silently mourned without the comfort of her family or friends, but she held on to God and found a way through the trial.

Over the next few months, Lily worked at a variety of part-time jobs, until she finally secured a job working for a customer service company making phone calls. The job offered her more hours and better pay, and she had Sabbaths off, which was one of her requirements, for she vowed to always uphold the Lord's fourth commandment.

Lily loved the Lord and was committed to supporting His church with her tithes and offerings, which she sent back to her home church. Lily also sent money home to her mother to help care for her medical needs—Nydia had been diagnosed with a heart disease.

With each paycheck, she put a little aside in hopes of fulfilling her dream of buying the Good Vision Farm. In hopes of making more money, Lily decided to invest in some real estate. She purchased a residential lot and set a mobile home on it. She had plans to clean the lot and put up a wood fence, but first she contracted with a survey company to put in the needed utilities. It was then that she discovered that the lot was very rocky and excavation was impossible. Lily contacted the seller regarding the problem with the land, but after a brief discussion, it became evident that she needed to seek the counsel of a lawyer.

A short legal battle ensued, but God blessed, and in the end, Lily received a significant amount of money from the company that sold her the land.

It seemed that it was the perfect opportunity to buy the Good Vision Farm. Lily wired the money to her family, and they approached to the owner of the farm and asked if he would be interested in selling the farm. Unfortunately, he turned them down.

Although separated by thousands of miles, Lily talked things over with her siblings, and they decided to buy a small farm in another region with hopes that someday things would change and they could sell the one farm and purchase their childhood farm.

Nydia enjoyed the companionship of Leonor, but because of her poor health, it became evident that Leonor could no longer take care of her mother. Lily made arrangements for a woman named Silvana to live with Mother and care for her every need. Then Lily announced that she planned to return home for Christmas, which was only a few months away.

Mother was very excited when she heard the news. "In only two months I will be home, Mother. We will enjoy a beautiful Christmas together," Lily said one evening while talking to her mother on the phone.

"Are you coming to stay?" Mother wanted to know.

"I am coming home for good, Mother. America has become like a second home to me, but my heart is still where my family is, and my mind is still filled with the sweet memories of my childhood. I promise you that I am coming back home, Mother."

A few weeks after this conversation, Nydia welcomed the Sabbath with her church family and friends. Marieta, the sister of one of their former employees, and Urucuia and Paloma enjoyed the Sabbath hours together with Nydia, as they were all sisters and brothers in Christ now, having been reunited after so many years apart.

Sunday dawned bright and cheerful, and Nydia enjoyed a fun-filled day surrounded by her grandchildren and children. Later that afternoon she returned to her home, although she walked a bit slower as the excitement of the day had worn her out. Silvana prepared a cup of tea for Nydia, but when she walked into the living room to give it to her, she found Nydia reclined on the sofa and suffering from a heart attack. She lifted Nydia's head and called for help. Then she said a prayer and asked the Lord to intervene according to His will. With that Nydia closed her eyes and took her last breath. She, too, along with her husband and her son, JuJu, were now waiting for the sound of the trumpet when the dead in Christ will rise.

Chapter 19

Lily took the news of her mother's death hard. Mother had been the main reason for returning to Brazil, but now she was gone. How Lily wished she had been able to see her again.

She cried and cried over the loss of her mother, but in the midst of her pain, she realized that what she was really crying for was heaven. She longed to go home and live with God in a place where there was to be no more death or suffering or sadness. Lily found encouragement in God's Word and His promises.

With the death of her mother, Lily had an even stronger desire to buy the Good Vision Farm, as it was the only legacy still remained that kept her attached to her family's heritage. Once again, Lily felt that it was a wise move to invest in real estate. This time she bought a piece of property at a government auction. She planned to build a house, sell it, and take the profits and head to Brazil, where she hoped she would have enough to purchase the farm.

Lily felt more confident in this real estate investment, because she figured it was through a government entity. Unfortunately, instead of placing her trust in God and seeking His will, she placed her trust in secular authority and monetary success, only to be disappointed when all of her money was lost. Lily tried to get her money back from the auction, since the government entity informed her that no one could build on the lot, even though they were the ones who sold it in the first place, but they would not give her her money. She decided to sue the government entity, but the lawsuit was denied again and again in the court system.

With no investment and no savings, Lily did not know what to do but return home to Brazil. She had longed to return with enough money to buy the farm, but that clearly was not going to happen. At that point and time, she simply longed to be home with people she loved and who loved her.

With her mind made up, she told her boss, Paul, who was director of the finance division, about her decision to go back home. She told him that she was leaving behind the piece of land that she couldn't build on or sell, because who would want to buy a piece of property that couldn't be built on. Paul was a polite man and a respected professional with a successful career. He was also a go-to person. He made it clear to his staff that if anyone had a question or a problem, he was available at any time to help. When Lily came to him about this problem and indicated that she felt it was best to return to Brazil, Paul offered to help her with the issue of the property. Unknown to Lily, Paul and his wife planned to purchase the land from her and deal with the legal issues to apply for a building permit.

With the issues over the property cleared up, there was nothing holding Lily back from going home. With a thankful heart to God for fixing her problems, Lily boarded the airplane and flew to the closest airport to her hometown. There she rented a car and drove to the Good Vision Farm.

Life had brought her full circle. She had been born on the farm, and now as an adult she was back. As she looked around at the bright blue sky, the prairie, and the river, she felt a sense of peace wash over her—she was home. This was where she belonged. She walked the short distance from where she had parked her car to the cashew tree, her faithful old friend. It towered above her like a permanent guardian watching over the farm.

As she sat under the cashew tree, she talked to her Best Friend. *God, I know that it is not by chance that I am here again on my family farm. I sense the goodness and greatness of Your presence here with me. You know that it has always been my desire to acquire this farm. Maybe the owner of the farm will continue to be stubborn and refuse to sell, maybe he will ask a very high price that I cannot afford, or maybe he has no intention of ever selling this farm, but I know that nothing is too hard for You. Your power and majesty is beyond comprehension, and at this moment, the mountains, the prairie, the river, and this cashew tree testify to your greatness and power. Humbly I come to You and ask You for one more miracle. Please give me back the farm. May the Holy Spirit work in the mind and heart of the owner and convince him to sell me the Good Vision Farm. If you choose to help me acquire the farm, I will let everyone know that You are a God of wonders who works in mysterious ways to provide for His children. I trust in Your love, power, mercy, grace, and faithfulness. You are in control. I thank you in advance for what you will do in my life. Amen.*

Lost in her own thoughts as she talked to God, Lily did not hear someone approach on horseback. She jumped when the man dismounted in front of her and asked, "Lady, who are you? And what are you doing on my property?"

"Who… who me? I am sorry, sir. My name is Lily. I apologize for coming onto your property uninvited, but I would really like to buy your farm."

"I'm sorry, but this farm is not for sale."

"Why not? I have this feeling that you would sell to me," Lily said.

"I do not have any intention of selling this farm. I just bought this farm a few months ago. What makes you think that I would sell this farm?"

"Please, sir, tell me, are you Mr. Dualdo, Jr.?"

"No, madam, I am not. He sold me this farm and moved to the capital city with his family."

"If I may ask, what is your name, sir?"

"Manuel Modesto, but you may call me Modesto."

"You see, sir, many years ago I lived here with my parents and siblings. My father was the first owner of this farm. As you can imagine, this farm means a lot to me. It is my family legacy, I …"

Modesto interrupted Lily and exclaimed, "You are Mr. Justo's daughter?"

"Yes, sir, I am. I am the seventh child born to Mr. Justo and Nydia."

"Ah! I see. So you want to buy the farm."

"Yes, I most certainly do. If we can settle on a reasonable price, I will pay you today once I exchange my U.S. dollars."

"There is no need to exchange currency. U.S. dollars will be just fine. This is certainly a surprise, and I must admit that this is a big decision, but I can see how much this means to you to own your family farm."

Lily held her breath as Modesto took his riding crop and wrote a figure in the dirt at their feet. It was a reasonable price that Lily eagerly accepted by taking a stick and writing "yes" in the dirt.

"OK, madam, meet me this afternoon at the title company and the property is yours."

Lily was home—she was finally home!

We invite you to view the complete
selection of titles we publish at:

www.TEACHServices.com

Please write or email us your praises, reactions,
or thoughts about this or any other book we publish at:

P.O. Box 954
Ringgold, GA 30736

info@TEACHServices.com

TEACH Services, Inc., titles may be purchased in bulk for
educational, business, fund-raising, or sales promotional use.
For information, please e-mail:

BulkSales@TEACHServices.com

Finally, if you are interested in seeing
your own book in print, please contact us at

publishing@TEACHServices.com

We would be happy to review your manuscript for free.

www.ingramcontent.com/pod-product-compliance
Lightning Source LLC
Chambersburg PA
CBHW080523110426
42742CB00017B/3217